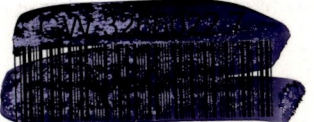

Heritage Trees
Wales

Archie Miles

GRAFFEG

About the author

A professional photographer for more than thirty-five years, Herefordshire based author Archie Miles has always had an abiding passion for landscape and natural history. A specialisation over the last twenty years has seen him carving a distinctive niche in the world of trees, and he works on a regular basis with both The Tree Council and the Woodland Trust. He has travelled the length and breadth of the British Isles to photograph many of the country's greatest and rarest trees as well as a huge diversity of woodland types.

Previous publications include *Silva – The Tree in Britain*, *The Malvern Hills – Travels through Elgar Country*, *The Malvern Hills and Westward*, *The Hidden Trees of Britain*. In 2004 he was principal photographer and art director for The Tree Council's *The Heritage Trees of Britain and Northern Ireland* and in 2006 undertook the same roles for *Heritage Trees of Scotland*. In 2006 he also wrote and photographed the tie-in book for a popular BBC2 TV series *The Trees that Made Britain*. In 2009 he wrote and photographed *A Walk in the Woods* for Woodland Trust.

Archie Miles

Right: A grove of perry pears set in the hillside above Llanvihangel-Ystern-Llewern.

Published by Graffeg
Copyright © Graffeg 2012
ISBN 9781905582495

Graffeg, 16 Neptune Court, Vanguard Way, Cardiff Bay CF24 5PJ Wales UK.
www.graffeg.com

For all other sources of archive images see Acknowledgements page.

The author and publishers are grateful for the generous support of Countryside Council for Wales and Forestry Commission Wales, which has made the publication of this book possible.

The publishers are also grateful to the Welsh Books Council for their financial support and marketing advice.

Designed and produced by Peter Gill & Associates
www.petergill.com

A CIP Catalogue record for this book is available from the British Library.

Contents

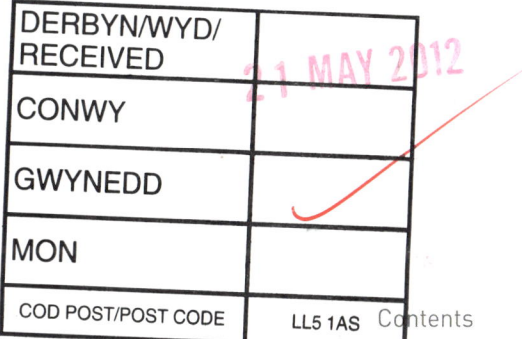

Foreword

Markers of time, guardians of biodiversity, subjects of folklore and repositories of history; the trees in this book have a place in the heritage of Wales comparable to its great eisteddfodau, towering fortifications and mines from which were brought forth gold, slate and coal.

Like all of these, heritage trees survive thanks to the individuals, past and present, who have kept the awareness of their importance alive. However, in the life of a tree, it takes only one person to neglect, mutilate or destroy it. In contrast to historic buildings and landscapes, safeguards specific to trees of heritage significance are not by design: many could be felled tomorrow without penalty. The value of these trees, these Green Monuments, is already formalised in other countries. This protection is known by various names, extended because of the undisputed historical, cultural and ecological value of these most amazing living things. Sadly, we are still some way from obtaining the acknowledgement and validation of their significance that will move the trees in this book, and others like them, to a similarly prominent position in the public eye.

The Tree Council and its member organisations are calling for a system which will safeguard historic trees, encourage their owners to look after them and provide information on management best practice. We launched the campaign for formal Green Monument status in 2003 and will continue it for as long as any of the UK nations fail to properly acknowledge this aspect of their heritage.

To raise awareness of these special trees, The Tree Council has brought together their stories in illustrated books that span the whole of the UK as well as directing the spotlight on Scotland. Now it is the turn of Wales, a nation whose trees include some fascinating and magnificent pieces of history and culture. In this new book, the focus is upon a Welsh tree heritage that may surprise, may raise curiosity to find out more, or may provoke indignation that this aspect of a proud heritage has gone largely unremarked for too long. One thing is certain: this oversight needs to be remedied so that, one day, these trees will be appreciated as Green Monuments in their own right.

Once you have seen the trees and their stories contained within these pages, I am sure you will agree that their recognition is long overdue.

Pauline Buchanan Black

Pauline Buchanan Black
Director-General, The Tree Council

Left: One of the Llanfihangel-nant-Melan Yews.

Introduction

The first step is to define exactly what a heritage tree might be and, in a world that has of late rather over-exploited the word 'heritage', how vital a part of our historical, social and natural culture these trees are. In 2006 James Ogilvie, writing the introduction for the *Heritage Trees of Scotland*, rather succinctly summed them up in this way:

'If the world of trees can be likened to the world of people, then heritage trees are the 'characters'. They're exceptional, extraordinary, uncommon and unexpected. Often they inspire wonder and awe; sometimes they instil humility and modesty; always they capture one's imagination. You might be surprised or even amazed by a heritage tree, but you'll never be indifferent.'

Above: Massive multi-stemmed Douglas fir in the arboretum at Golden Grove – reputedly planted in the 1860s.
Left: Dinefwr Park oaks.

This applies no less to special trees in Wales, indeed universally to heritage trees. Show almost anyone one of these trees and defy them not to be moved in some way; and it's not just the sheer scale or outlandish forms of so many of them, it's also the stories and traditions they carry with them. They provoke a sense of intrigue; the questions of who planted them, and why, and that romantic curiosity of wondering just what these trees may have witnessed throughout their many centuries of life.

And yet, how does one recognise a heritage tree? Like many things there is an element of subjectivity here. An ancient oak or yew may seem an obvious candidate, but then one might consider tiny trees growing from cliffs or exotic specimens in parks and gardens. Some trees are obviously special due to their immense age or vast size; other trees, sometimes of no great stature, come with wonderful stories; but there are also those which are just very rare or manifest in some strange form.

Yew trees of the greatest magnitude fall into roughly calculated age parameters of 1,500 – 3,000 years, a timeline that no other native species can aspire to. Each and every yew has a very distinct, unique character, a life span steeped in mystery, taking its own very individual path down the millennia. These are maverick trees, growing in fits and starts, turning in on themselves, boles and boughs fusing together, layering themselves or throwing down aerial roots. Their forms confuse us as much as their place in our cultural and spiritual world. History tells us that they have long been venerated, even before the advent of Christianity, but the last 1,500 years has seen them absorbed and accepted on sites of Christian worship. In Wales there also appears to be much evidence of their association with early saint cells. The wealth of incredible yews in Wales, particularly along the border with England, is admirably demonstrated within these pages.

Oaks, of course, are the iconic British tree; firm, durable, dependable, the 'wooden walls' of the nation as John Evelyn pronounced them. A few true giants still grow in Wales, although archive material reveals that many more were around in the nineteenth century. The greatest of all is the Pontfadog Oak in the Ceiriog Valley, near Chirk: with its impressive girth of over 42 feet (12.8 metres) it could easily be 1,000 years old, and perhaps as much as 1,200 years. Few oaks will make it this far and, sadly, the Pontfadog Oak is showing signs of collapse, so its long-term future may be in doubt. Again, ancient oaks do simply look the part of a heritage tree – squat, rugged geometry with deeply fissured bark, and thumping great lateral boughs. A long history of regular pollarding has helped them to thrive, when a maiden oak of lesser years would normally have matured and died.

Much like yews, the longevity of oaks has secured them a role as boundary trees for many centuries, sometimes to the point where they became focal points for a community, either for celebrations or ceremonies – most particularly those gospel oaks where the gospel was preached during the annual beating of the bounds of the parish.

At the other end of the heritage tree scale are the small and the rare, and very often these are the trees which grow in some of the most inhospitable locations. Much research has been done over the last few years by the botanists and dendrologists of the National Museum Wales into the whitebeam genus. Discoveries of new species have come almost every year just lately, and many of these are only indigenous to Wales, and incredibly localised to boot. The trees are found growing almost exclusively from remote and sheer rock faces (usually limestone), but they are of diminutive size, seldom more than 20 feet high. At best there may be 200–300 specimens of a species. At worst, in the case of Ley's whitebeam, only 13 trees survive in the wild. An intriguing colony of juniper grows on Ramsey Island, off the Pembrokeshire coast – they are small, unremarkable looking little clumps clinging to the steep cliffs, but their story and their history is phenomenal. The record for the shortest heritage tree (not just in this book, but perhaps in the whole of Wales), must go to the prostrate blackthorn of Aberystwyth, although in extent it is huge.

Dilapidated beech coppice stool in Silent Valley, Ebbw Vale.

Of course, the hand of man has also helped to shape many different heritage trees as well as the landscapes in which they are found. The deer parks of Dinefwr and Powis were managed and treasured by a succession of aristocratic owners who combined the love of the chase with an admiration for the splendour of their own personal landscapes, whether natural or faux-natural, ensuring a long legacy of fine old broadleaf pollards.

Large estates planted their avenues. Some survive, but many more fell foul of the caprices of landscape fashion. Similar vicissitudes were visited on topiary, a vogue for which the pendulum of taste has swung back and forth several times. In some respects it is remarkable that anything survived at all, but Powis Castle yews still stand proud.

Parks and gardens are wonderful repositories of the imported exotics of the eighteenth and nineteenth centuries. As soon as new species arrived on British shores, a race ensued to see who could be the first to plant them and, more's the point, show them off with some smug pride to neighbours and guests. Many an arboretum was established in the pleasure grounds of the stately houses of Wales. Tragically, some were lost when the estates became too onerous to maintain, but others have survived with their splendid collections intact. Golden Grove, near Llandeilo, presents a magical example which was on the cusp of decline and disappearance when the grand house was closed down. Fortunately, the local council saw the significance and potential of the site and have resurrected and maintained the arboretum for public enjoyment. Here are massive conifers, planted in their Victorian heyday when the thrill of these exotic arrivals was at its height. When William Hill, gardener to the Cawdor family, planted these trees he must have had no concept whatsoever that they might one day become heritage trees, but they most assuredly are since they tell an important chapter in the evolution of a nation's tree story. Without realising it, these tree planters were creating a new aspect to the nation's tree heritage. Today we can look at the exotic plantings of the last 200 years and learn much about how well these aliens have adapted to their new homes, taking that knowledge and using it wisely when we plant the same trees for the future. Most parks on private estates are still very much off-limits to the public, but just occasionally they are open under the National Gardens Scheme. In the centre of Cardiff is one park and arboretum boasting more than 2,000 trees that has most definitely been in the public domain since 1947, when the 5th Marquess of Bute presented it to Cardiff Council.

One of the most unlikely sources of heritage trees has proved to be traditional orchards. These may be found in various parts of Wales, although historically the epicentre has long been recognised as Monmouthshire. A brief exploration of the county's old orchards has barely scratched the surface, yet it has been enough to show that there is a wealth of very special, possibly unique varieties of fruit trees out there. Many are huge specimens – some of the pears in particular may be well in excess of 200 years old – but what also makes these trees special are the orchard habitats around them, little changed for many decades. Habitat is a hugely important facet of most heritage trees, whether it be the hedgerows, parklands or woodlands where they have survived or, indeed, the habitats they provide within and upon themselves for invertebrates, birds, bats, and a rich variety of mosses, ferns and lichens.

From the most ancient of yews wedged solidly and stately in its churchyard haunt to the most miniscule, slightly scraggy, whitebeam clinging tenaciously to a windswept crag: all of the subjects within this book are worthy heritage

Llangollen Whitebeam

trees. However many more go unnoticed, unrecorded and, perhaps worryingly, unprotected. Ultimately, at present, the secure future of the majority of heritage trees relies upon the goodwill of the owners. It seems bizarre that there are listed buildings and listed landscapes, yet our heritage trees, in many cases much older and more threatened than any of these, have next to no protection.

Most private owners respect and treasure those green monuments that are in their safekeeping. The Ty Mawr Oak, tucked away on a private estate, was something of a discovery for me. Of course, the landowners have held the tree in great affection for several generations, but for a visitor talking about trees for an hour or two with people who obviously love all their trees, it was simply an insight into how, very quietly, so many private estates in Wales are caring for their veteran and ancient trees. Often their stewardship is done in complete isolation from other owners, with little or no specialist technical advice or financial assistance. Anyone who is prepared to care for an ancient tree rather than felling it because it might present a health and safety hazard is to be applauded, but tree owners need advice and support.

Above: One of the magnificent wild cherries in spring at Tan-y-Pistyll.
Left: The Alltmawr Yew

However, some trees in rural areas may be under pressure from agricultural practise, with issues such as soil compaction from livestock, deep ploughing near tree roots (often root systems extend a lot further than might be expected), and misuse or overuse of agrichemicals, bearing in mind most ancient trees have spent the bulk of their lifespan without synthetic chemistry in their water supply. There are further concerns for ancient trees in public spaces; pressures of urban development, litigation associated with accidents caused by failure of the tree or subsidence to property, well-meaning yet damaging maintenance, as well as mindless vandalism. Even the effects of trampling feet from hordes of adoring fans have the potential to cause stress to root systems due to soil compaction. Add to this the potential effects of pollution, pests and diseases, as well as the imponderable element of climate change, and it begins to look like an uphill battle for the trees.

The Tree Council and its member organisations have worked hard over the last few years to raise the profile of heritage trees throughout Britain. The public have engaged, masses of data has been gathered, but now there needs to be something new to carry this interest and information forward with some sense of continuity and clout. If The Tree Council's 'Green Monument Campaign' can gain political approval and legislative adoption, offering practical support with a technical network and grant funding opportunities, then we will have better opportunities in the future to look after our heritage trees.

Long Lost Heritage Trees

Exploring a variety of archives uncovers an interesting array of images of historic trees usually, but not always, long gone, as well as some extremely detailed accounts from a variety of observers. It makes one realise that the fascination with heritage trees, particularly those with great dimensions and antiquity as well as those with historic connections, is not some late twentieth-century craze; for well over 200 years people have been captivated by extraordinary trees.

The earliest mention of specific trees of interest in Wales may be found in the mid-sixteenth century writings of John Leland, who was moved by the 39 remarkable yew trees then growing at Strata Florida Abbey (see p.160). In the eighteenth century, writers, naturalists and travellers such as the Honourable Daines Barrington, Thomas Pennant and Peter Collinson, a leading dendrologist of the period, were recording some of the most remarkable trees in Britain. Thomas Pennant (1726–1798), born and raised in Flintshire, and often described as 'The Father of Cambrian Tourists,' made three major tours of Wales – he account of the first published in 1778, and the subsequent two in 1791.

Above: The Newcastle
Oak, Monmouth, 1815 –
a delightful watercolour
by an unknown artist.
Left: The Shordley Oak
from J. C. Loudon's
*Arboretum et Fruticetum
Britannicum* of 1838.

He doesn't make many references to specific trees, but those he does remark upon clearly made an impression (see Mallwyd Yew p.176).

In fact most trees, and particularly yews, begin to receive mentions in the 1830s and 1840s in Samuel Lewis's frequent editions of *A Topographical Dictionary of Wales*. The early nineteenth century was a period when travelling and tourism was on the increase, something that the arrival of the railways would also accelerate throughout the Victorian age. Numerous publishers and writers prepared guides, both national and local, to satisfy the thirst for tourist information. The 1820s and 1830s also saw a dramatic upsurge in the production of engravings and lithographic prints which, in a pre-photographic era, became wonderful mementoes of tourist travels. Whilst most of these prints depict castles, abbeys and the great houses of the day, a few artists and publishers saw the potential for pictures of landscapes and, occasionally, the most impressive trees. Some of these remarkable historic documents have survived the last 200 years, but they are rare. For some reason early depictions of Welsh trees are few and far between. Two of the most revered nineteenth-century books on trees seem to have almost completely skirted around the largest and most historic Welsh trees. Jacob George Strutt published his stunning *Sylva Britannica*, an illustrated homage to Britain's great trees, in 1820 (a subsequent smaller version published in 1830), but

Above: This engraving of a grotesque alder on the River Taff, near Pontypridd, appeared in the Agricultural Gazette in 1874, reflecting the Victorian fascination with the weird and wonderful aspects of nature.

there are no Welsh trees. John Claudius Loudon published *Arboretum et Fruticetum Britannicum* in 1838, and actually employed quite a few of Strutt's illustrations, yet also managed to mention relatively few important Welsh trees. The Mamhilad Yew is featured, with a fine little engraving included (see p.108), the Llanthewy Vach Yew, near Caerleon (sadly, no more), The Gresford Yew (see p.196) and the briefest of mentions for Strata Florida (see p.160).

Several writers recall the Golynos Oak (see p.26), famous for its astounding volume of timber, and the Nannau Oak (see p.30), infamous for its story of a dastardly deed. Although Loudon only provides the tiniest of woodcuts of the Nannau Oak and the Shordley Oak, he does relay some accounts of remarkable Welsh oaks that had been sent to him by correspondents.

L.W. Dillwyn, Esq., M.P. wrote of the Sketty Oak (on the western outskirts of Swansea), 'This tree grows at Lower Sketty, about 2 miles from my house. When I first came into the neighbourhood, in 1802, it was a magnificent tree; but, a few years afterwards, it was much damaged by lightning; and one of the main branches, within these 3 or 4 years, has been torn off by a storm. The trunk is quite hollow with a circumference of 37 feet 9 inches at the base; and it measures 24 feet 2 inches at 4 feet 6 inches from the ground, before any

NANNAU OAK, OR THE SPIRIT'S BLASTED TREE.

Above: Nannau Oak, or
The Spirit's Blasted Tree
from *English Forests
and Forest Trees* 1853.

T.H.Thomas del.-et-lith

T.Way, imp.

OAK (Quercus pedunculata) HENSOL CASTLE, NEAR CARDIFF.
Smallest Girth, 11 ft, Spread, 110 ft.

T.H.Thomas del.-et-lith.

T.Way, imp.

THE WYCH ELM, COTTRELL, NEAR CARDIFF.
Girth at 5 ft from ground 21 ft.

The "Gospel" Oak at Llanllugan, under which Howel Harris preached about 1743.

of the enlargement occasioned by the branches begins.' Mr. Dillwyn also offers a description of another great tree – the Lanelay Oak, a slightly larger tree growing a mile and a half from Llantrisant, which was, '38 feet 6 inches around the base, and 27 feet 2 inches at 3 feet from the ground,' although this tree was in a greatly decayed state. Apart from a very rough sketch of the Sketty Oak in the Swansea Museum this is all we know of these trees. However, without these wonderfully detailed accounts, such giants would have run their allotted spans and disappeared unrecorded; heritage tree voids of history.

Although the Victorians were avid planters of all types of trees, the main focus on what we would understand as heritage trees was with the massive, celebrated native species, but principally oak. The great conifers we admire today had barely put down roots, so it's only in recent years they have attracted celebrity status. A glance at a list of famous British trees reveals dozens with links to Queen Victoria – either those planted or used to celebrate her accession (see Caeryder Oak p.98), those she planted herself, those she visited, or simply the ones that she admired, much like the massive Queen's Oak on the Wynnstay Estate near Ruabon (see p.25). However, even Victoria could not rival the number of trees associated with Queen Elizabeth I.

In the handwritten annotations on the postcard: 28/3/04 — JWH — TREDEGAR PARK — Oak Trees. — Huxtable Bros

Above: These old oak pollards on a conveniently dated postcard from 1904 stood in Tredegar Park, near Newport, Monmouthshire. Today the old deer park, originally laid out shortly after 1664 still exists, including one broad avenue of old oaks.

In the 1870s T.H. Thomas compiled his *Silva Silurica* – a very personal collection of images and accounts of the most remarkable trees of Monmouthshire and Glamorgan. Most of them, such as the Llantarnum Oak, the Newbridge-on-Usk Oak, and the Hensol Oak are long gone, although Thomas was obviously awestruck by this last tree. 'I cannot hope to convey in words the wonderful character of this tree. I have seen nothing at all to equal it ... A vast and grotesque trunk bears, in some aspects, a resemblance to some fantastic Eastern or Mexican idol... To stand under the circuit of branches and to look around, is to seem encircled by a writhing mass of pythons, and shows us in living form "such stuff as dreams are made of."' He mentions the Caeryder Oak (see p.98) which at that date was still very much, 'an almost perfect example of a first-class tree of the short-stemmed wide-spreading type of growth,' going on to detail its every dimension. Thomas was an accomplished artist and sketched some delightful studies, most of them unique records of notable trees. He mentions an English elm in the Plaisance of Raglan Castle, which was lost in 1876, and had a girth of 21 feet (6.4 metres) at 2 feet from the ground – a stunning tree without doubt; also massive wych elms at Llanarvon, near Cwmbran, and another in Cottrell Park, near Cardiff, both around 30 feet (9.14 metres) in girth at ground level. In 1875 Thomas was

Above: This remarkable tree is a huge walnut in Cam-yr-Alyn Parc at Rossett, near Wrexham. It was photographed by Elwes and Henry during their early twentieth-century tour of Britain in search of the nation's finest trees for their *Trees of Great Britain and Ireland.*

taken down to Cottrell Park, but ruefully recalls, 'on our arrival we were dismayed to find that the grand branches had been wrenched away by winds, and we had only the trunk, bound by an iron girdle, to study.' He still managed to make a splendid sketch of the remains, but the artist's tale of woe has been a familiar thread in my own photography of trees. When you hear of an amazing tree go and see it straight away!

During the latter half of the nineteenth century photography developed rapidly into a means by which almost everyone could record the world about them without necessarily having great artistic skills. However, few people seem to have taken much notice of the great trees all about them. Perhaps there were just too many far more interesting things on which to focus. Fortunately, one John Thomas, about whom little is known, did take it upon himself to record some important trees from the 1860s through to the 1880s, copies of which have very fortunately come to rest in the National Library of Wales (see the Peace Tree, p.192).

At the beginning of the twentieth century Henry John Elwes and Augustine Henry privately published their *Trees of Great Britain and Ireland* – a grand, seven volume work which was the most comprehensive book on trees since

The "Rock" Ash, Llanbedr.

The "Oak" at Pontfadog
Largest Oak Tree in the United-
Kingdom, 17 yards round

Above: The Rock Ash, Llanbedr and Pontfadog Oak Edwardian postcards.
Opposite / top: The Queen's Oak, on the Wynnstay Estate, near Ruabon.
Right: Edwardian postcard celebrating a rather unusual rural novelty – the Donkey's Tree Stable, Usk.

Loudon and probably has yet to be surpassed. They visited many estates throughout Britain and a few in Wales are extremely well documented – notably Powis – and there are a handful of beautiful photogravure plates of some exceptional Welsh trees.

However, while photographs of special trees in Wales are relatively thin on the ground, there were a few publishers busily exploiting one of the biggest phenomena of the Edwardian period – the picture postcard – as they reckoned that a few famous trees had real commercial potential with the tourist markets. The Pontfadog Oak (see p.208) appears on several postcards, but, considering it claimed to be the biggest oak in the United Kingdom, they are still not easy to find today, particularly when compared with the plethora of cards made of the famous Major Oak in Sherwood Forest. With its wealth of massive yew trees, again Welsh examples on cards are almost non-existent apart from the Strata Florida Yew. Some quite obscure tree pictures were

THE QUEENS TREE, RUABON (LARGEST TREE IN WALES.)

actually made into postcards, about which almost nothing can be discovered. But then this does make them incredibly important documents, intriguing windows on the past, recording a little slice of social history, not of earth-shattering proportions perhaps, but trees which once meant something to someone; a time and place, momentous or not, forgotten or lost.

Trees will not live forever, so today we are still witnessing the passing of some of these ancients. The Caeryder Oak is but a bleached carcass, and the Millennium Derwen looks likely to follow soon. At least there is little chance these days of mighty trees like the old Golynos Oak being felled for their timber, but time and the elements will continue to take their toll. The task now is to identify and care for the heritage trees of the future.

THE DONKEY'S TREE STABLE, USK, MONMOUTHSHIRE.

Golynos Oak

1 Map D6

The great Golynos (or Gelonos) Oak, is a tree that sadly no longer stands. However the wonderfully detailed account of its felling in an era when oak timber was at a premium for shipbuilding, and oak bark, used in the process of tanning leather, was often more valuable than the timber itself, gives a fascinating insight into the timber trade of 200 years ago.

The ubiquitous John Claudius Loudon in his *Arboretum et Fruticetum Britannicum* of 1838 provides a superbly detailed account of the tree's commercial value, its felling and conversion:

'...often cited as an example of vast ligneous production.'

'The Gelonos Oak, felled in Monmouthshire, AD 1810, has been often cited as an example of vast ligneous production. The bark was sold by the merchant for the scarcely credible sum of £200. This oak was purchased by Mr. Thomas Harrison for 100 guineas, under the apprehension of its being unsound; but Burnet tells us that it was resold, while still standing, for £405; and that the cost of converting it was £82; amounting altogether to £487: it was subsequently resold for £675. There were at least 400 rings or traces of annual growth, within its mighty trunk.

The Gelonos Oak, which was cut down in 1810, grew about 4 miles from Newport, in Monmouthshire [it actually grew on Fair Oak Farm at Bassaleg, now the site of the club house of Newport Golf Club]. The main trunk was 10 feet. long, and produced 450 cubic feet of timber; 1 limb, 355 feet.; 1 ditto, 472 feet.; 1 ditto, 113 feet; and 6 other limbs, of inferior size, averaged 93 feet. each; making a total of 2,426 cubic feet of convertible timber. The bark was estimated at 6 tons; but, as some of the very heavy body bark was stolen out of the barge at Newport, the exact weight is not known. Five men were 20 days stripping and cutting down this tree; and two sawyers were 5 months converting it, without losing a day, Sundays excepted. The main trunk was 9 and a half feet in diameter [equating to a girth of about 31 feet]; and, in sawing it through, a stone was discovered 6 feet from the ground, above a yard in the body of the tree, through which the saw cut. The stone was about 6 inches in diameter, and was completely shut in; but around it there was not the least symptom of decay. The rings in the but were carefully counted, and

amounted to upwards of four hundred in number; a convincing proof that this tree was in an improving state for upwards of four hundred years; and, as the ends of some of its branches were decayed, and had dropped off, it is presumed that it had stood a great number of years after it had attained maturity. (ref. *Literary Panorama* for August, 1815; and the *Gentleman's Magazine* for October 1817).'

Much of the timber went to the Royal Navy Dockyard at Plymouth, but the tree was obviously something of a celebrity before it was felled, as several fine engravings and lithographs from the period attest; but it is uncertain whether anything over and above its great size attracted this notability. The thought that anyone today could possibly consider felling such a splendid old oak doesn't bear thinking about, but attitudes to what would now be considered a heritage tree, as well as the commercial rewards from a relentlessly demanding navy, were very different 200 years ago.

Merlin's Oak

2 Map B5

Many are the ancient monuments and landscape features that have traditionally been romanticised by local communities; good yarns, even superstitions, handed down from one generation to the next, with the slenderest of historical threads to keep them alive. From the late eighteenth century, when tourism effectively began, these were the tales that often attracted visitors to certain places, so a strong line in folk tradition was also good for the local economy.

There has been a long-standing association between the town of Carmarthen and Merlin, the wizard of Arthurian legend. Some say that the town's name Caerfyrddin is a corruption of the fort of Myrddin (Merlin), while others believe that because the town is much older than the first mention of Merlin, in the writings of Geoffrey of Monmouth in the twelfth century, the association is the other way around. It matters not, for the link has been happily perpetuated to this day.

In the nineteenth century an oak tree grew at the corner of Priory Street and Oak Lane, which acquired the name of Merlin's Oak (sometimes Priory Oak), based on the belief that the boy Merlin, whilst playing in the tree, heard that it was due to be chopped down. Infuriated, he is supposed to have cast a spell that should anything untoward happen to his favourite tree then disaster would befall the town; most particularly that, following this act of vandalism, the town would flood or be drowned (see verse on postcard opposite).

It is believed that the oak was planted around 1660 by a local schoolmaster to celebrate the restoration of King Charles II to the throne of England; so unless this was a replacement of a much earlier tree the Merlin connection has already vaporised. There is little or no mention of the tree until the mid-nineteenth century when a local man, apparently annoyed by all the people who were forever gathering at the tree, decided to poison it. This appears to have worked and it was said to have died by 1856.

However, ploughing through the many websites that mention this tree, a conundrum has arisen. A Victorian sepia photograph, clearly of the correct location, shows a group of people beneath a small, and decidedly alive, oak tree. If the tree was then about 200 years old then it appears to be remarkably small. Might it be a fragment of a once much larger tree? It is feasible that this photograph is earlier than 1856, but the suspicion is that it is a little later. Frustratingly, even with the kind help of the people who manage the website, neither the photograph nor its owners can be traced.

Right: A 1920s postcard from the Francis Frith Company shows the Merlin's oak stump on its concrete pedestal.

Below: The puzzling nineteenth century photograph of Merlin's Oak. Was this taken prior to 1856, or was the tree poisoned some time after this?

Carmarthen, Old Oak

When Priory Oak shall tumble down
Then will fall Carmarthen Town.
Merlin's Prophecy.

Certainly by the twentieth century the old oak was entirely dead, although, as numerous postcards show, it was well and truly wedged in place with a giant block of concrete and surrounded by a small, iron railing. The prophecy had not been forgotten. In 1951 a branch broke off, and this fragment is preserved in the County Museum. In 1978 it was deemed to be dangerous and so, with some misgivings perhaps, it was carefully taken down and removed to St. Peter's Civic Hall in Nott Square. Whether the prophecy was fulfilled or simply that extreme climatic conditions prevailed the following year is a moot point, but in 1979 Carmarthen suffered some of its worst ever flooding. Fortunately though, it was not the end for the town.

Nannau Oak

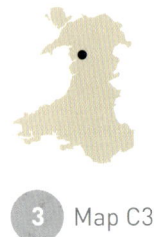

3 Map C3

Few trees in the land can evoke such bloodthirsty and terrifying images as the infamous Nannau Oak, which once grew on the wild hills of the Nannau Estate near Dolgellau. Almost exactly 200 years since it fell, it remains prominent in Welsh folklore.

There are many mentions of the tree and its gruesome story in several early nineteenth-century books, but perhaps the most comprehensive gathering of references to the tree's inauspicious past are detailed in *The Every-Day Book* by William Hone in 1830.

A dramatic stanza from the writings of Mrs. Radcliffe sets the scene:

> It stood alone, a wither'd oak
> Its shadow fled, its branches broke;
> Its riven trunk was knotted round,
> Its gnarled roots o'erspread the ground
> Honours that were from tempests won,
> In generations long since gone,
> A scanty foliage yet was seen,
> Wreathing its hoary brows with green,
> Like to a crown of victory
> On some old warrior's forehead grey,
> And, as it stood, it seem'd to speak
> To winter winds in murmurs weak,
> Of times that long had passed it by
> And left it desolate, to sigh
> Of what it was, and seem'd to wail,
> A shadeless spectre, shapeless, pale.

As history relates there was some enmity between Owain Glyndŵr and his cousin Howel Sele, Lord of Nannau. Glyndŵr, who laid claim to the throne of Wales, was passionately opposed to the invading armies of Henry IV and knew that Howel Sele, if not blatantly in league with the House of Lancaster, had leanings towards the English monarchy. This infuriated Glyndŵr and in 1404 he made it his business to visit Nannau to thrash out their differences. It is said that the Abbot of Cymmer brought the two men together in hopes of a reconciliation and hence, with peace apparently brokered, the two men vowed to hunt together. However all was not well. It is said that Owain spied a doe feeding and remarked to Howel that this should be a fine mark for him.

WITHIN THE TRUNK OF THIS VENERABLE OAK (ACCORDING TO WELCH TRADITION) THE BODY OF HOWEL SELE, A POWERFUL CHIEFTAIN, RESIDING AT NANNAU, IN MERIONETHSHIRE, WAS IMMURED, BY ORDER OF HIS RIVAL OWEN GLYNDWR.—*See PENNANT, Vol. I. p.* 348.

THE ORIGINAL SKETCH FROM WHICH THIS ETCHING IS MADE, WAS DRAWN FROM NATURE ON THE 27TH DAY OF JULY, 1813, BY SIR RICHARD COLT HOARE, BART. AND ON THE SAME NIGHT, THIS AGED TREE FELL TO THE GROUND. IT WAS SITUATED WITHIN THE KITCHEN GARDEN WALLS OF SIR ROBERT WILLIAMS VAUGHAN, BART. AT NANNAU, NEAR DOLGELLE.

Howel bent his bow, aimed at the doe, but at the last moment turned and let fly his arrow at Owain's breast. Fortunately the armour beneath his clothes saved him from harm but enraged by this treachery Glyndŵr slew Howel Sele and burnt his house. Then, with the assistance of his companion Madoc, Glyndŵr concealed the body in the hollow oak. They then hurried away from Nannau, as they knew that Howel Sele's family and would soon send out a search party. Search they did, but nothing was found of their slain lord.

Forty years later Glyndŵr, on his deathbed beseeched Madoc to return to Nannau to reveal the fate of Howel Sele to his family. A long poem entitled 'The Spirit's Blasted Tree' relates the whole tragic tale, as if narrated by Madoc. At the time of the dark deed he notes:

Above: A silver-mounted oak goblet made from the timber of the fallen Nannau Oak.
The silver shield on the front is engraved with a rendition of the Colt Hoare drawing of the tree.

> I marked a broad and blasted oak,
> Scorched by the lightning's livid glare
> Hollow its stem from branch to root,
> And all its shrivelled arms were bare.
>
> Be this, I cried, his proper grave! –
> (The thought in me was deadly sin.)
> Aloft we raised the hapless chief,
> And dropped his bleeding corpse within.

Upon his return to Nannau, Madoc takes Howel Sele's horror-struck wife and her retinue to the fateful resting place.

> He led them near the blasted oak,
> Then, conscious, from the scene withdrew;
> The peasant's work with trembling haste,
> And lay the whitened bones to view! –
>
> Back they recoiled! – the right hand still,
> Contracted, grasped a rusty sword;
> Which erst in many a battle gleamed,
> And proudly decked their slaughtered lord.

The image is stark and horrendous, and understandably leads to the oak's ghastly, haunted reputation. The traveller Thomas Pennant, visiting in the late eighteenth century, describes it with some eloquence:

'On the road side is a venerable oak in its last stage of decay, and pierced by age into the form of a gothic arch; yet its present growth is twenty-seven feet and a half. The name is very classical, 'Derwen Ceubren yr Ellyll,' 'the hollow oak, the haunt of demons. How often has not warm fancy seen the fairy tribe revel round its trunk! or may not the visionary eye have seen the Hamadryad burst from the bark of its coeval tree.'

Ceubren yr Ellyll,
THE SPIRIT'S BLASTED TREE.

All nations have their omens drear,
Their legions wild of woe and fear,
To Cambria look—the peasant see,
Bethink him of Glendowerdy,
And shun " the spirit's Blasted Tree."

Marmion.

Remarkably, detailed accounts relate that the old oak finally fell on the night of 27–28 July 1813, immediately after the artist Sir Richard Colt Hoare had made a sketch of the venerable tree. Various etchings and engravings, mainly derived from this image, were published of the old tree, versions of which appear as prints and illustrations in several books of the period.

The fall of the tree was not the end of the story, for the timber was taken and crafted into numerous beautiful items of treen – notably a set of six superb silver-mounted acorn-shaped cups (hallmarked London 1816) inscribed 'Ceubren yr Ellyll a Syrthiodd I lawr yr 28 ain O Orphenaf 1813' (The Hollow Tree of the Demon which fell on the 28 July 1813), as well as a superb silver-mounted oak table seal (London 1817). These items were reputedly used as part of the celebrations for the coming of age of Robert Williams Vaughan of Nannau, a direct descendant of Howel Sele, on June 25th 1824. Some of these beautiful pieces were eventually acquired by the National Museum Wales, where they reside to this day.

The Nannau Estate survives to this day and a Cadw report reveals that a pillar in the old kitchen garden is supposed to mark the spot where the tree once stood. On a map of 1889 a sundial was marked upon the spot, but that has now gone. Images from antiquity and the vivid accounts of its sad story will forever keep this tree alive in Welsh folklore.

Discoed Yew

4 Map D4

Above: The yew in 1997 shortly after being relieved of its burden of ivy, although many of the dead stems had still to be cleared out of the tree.

To the north-west of Presteigne, on the south side of the Lugg Valley, lies the tiny hamlet of Discoed. In the churchyard of St. Michael two ancient yews flourish – a female tree with a girth of 22 feet (6.7 metres) and an astonishing male tree with a girth of 37 feet (11.2 metres) at 3 feet above ground level, making it, arguably, the largest yew in the whole of Wales. Only the monstrous yew at Llangernyw (see p.186) in north Wales comes close to this at 36 feet (10.97 metres).

This great yew (*Taxus baccata*) must have been a significant landmark in the valley long before the advent of Christianity, although widespread claims that it could be 5,000 years old seem somewhat excessive. Some observers believe that it may be no more than 1,400–1,500 years old, and coeval with the founding of the first church here, which itself may have been the result of a saint cell. Wells are often indicators of these cells and, in line with this, a spring fed well still flows near the north gate of the church. There are many proponents for the planting of yews to signal sacred Christian sites as well as landmarks to indicate the source of pure water around this time. However, the circular form of this churchyard probably indicates a pre-Christian site, and these cultures are known to have venerated yew trees, so with a girth which heralds a more realistic age of 2,000–2,500 years this could easily have been a significant tree to Iron Age people.

'...arguably the largest yew in the whole of Wales.'

Until fairly recent times the great tree was festooned with ivy, but, thankfully, most of this has been removed. Not only can the beautiful, rugged form of the ancient yew now be viewed to full advantage, but the risk of increased weight to old boughs and the potential of dense growth in the canopy, creating an adverse windsail effect in high winds, has been averted.

In spring the grass beneath the tree becomes a carpet of gold when the delicate little wild daffodils burst forth; well worth the short detour from the Offa's Dyke Path, which traverses the valley just a few hundred yards further west. It seems highly likely that when King Offa's men were excavating their great earthwork in the eighth century the Discoed Yew was already a substantial tree.

Offa's Dyke Oaks

5 Map D2 / D4

In 2011 the Offa's Dyke Path celebrated its 40th birthday, although the existence of the Dyke itself can be traced back to the late eighth century when King Offa ordered its construction, or so we are told in a reference about 100 years later in the writings of Asser, Bishop of Sherborne. Many scholars think it strange that there are no contemporary records of such a massive undertaking, but undoubtedly Offa was the first ruler with sufficient influence to organise such an earthwork.

Fine old oaks on Offa's
Dyke where it runs
through the Ceiriog
Valley below
Chirk Castle.
Pages 38–39: Huge
old oak on Offa's Dyke
above the Lugg Valley
near Discoed.

'Large trees have been boundary markers, certainly as far back as the eighth century...'

Along the Path's 177 mile length there still remain some parts of the ancient alignment that have all the hallmarks of a substantial defensive structure – a huge bank, sometimes as high as 25 feet, with a deep ditch running along its western side – while other sections may just be the equivalent of shallow wood or hedge banks; sometimes the formation even peters out altogether, giving rise to debate about its true location.

The borders of England and Wales have altered many times down the centuries, but sections of the Dyke will have held a defining role for much of the time. Large trees have served as boundary markers certainly as far back as the eighth century (as early documents attest) and it is unlikely, of course, that any of these trees survive today. There are theories that hollies and yews might previously have marked the Welsh borders, and some of those early yews might just still exist, particularly in places like the lower Wye Valley.

Today, among the most impressive trees to be discovered along the Path are some magnificent oaks. For the last three years Rob McBride, aka The Tree Hunter, stalwart of the 'Ancient Tree Hunt', has been walking every last bit of Offa's Dyke, mapping, measuring and recording every detail of all the ancient trees that he can find on or around it. On the northern part of the Path he has of course promoted the increasingly famous Great Oak at the Gates of the Dead in the Ceiriog Valley (see p.210), but a short stretch away from this, up in the parkland of Chirk Castle, are dozens more wonderful old oaks, mainly between 200 and 300 years old. A well-defined section of the Path runs through the park and bears several impressive oaks.

Llanfihangel-nant-Melan Yews

6 Map D4

Above: A Llanfihangel-nant-Melan gravestone depicts a grave beneath a yew tree.

The tiny hamlet of Llanfihangel-nant-Melan, which nestles around the busy A44, midway between Kington and Llandrindod Wells, might appear to have very little of interest to make a passing visitor pause on their journey across the border. However, a splendid collection of fine yew trees around the modest church of St. Michael assures a fascinating interlude.

Llanfihangel-nant-Melan translates as 'the church of St. Michael at the Mill Brook', and in 1833 Samuel Lewis's account of the village seems anything but notable:

'The surface is undulating; the hills are finely formed and of pleasing aspect, and the grounds in the lower part of the parish are richly clothed in wood. The surrounding scenery is pleasingly varied; and from the higher grounds are some interesting views, extending over the adjacent country.'

This would have been before the 1846 rebuilding of the church in the Norman Revival style, replacing an unremarkable earlier building. The origins of the first church on this site are believed to reach back to the thirteenth century. Lewis makes absolutely no mention of the yew trees. In 1868 *The National Gazetteer* does however make passing reference to the church, 'shaded by ancient yew trees.'

Five yews still thrive in a semicircle around the southern side of the church, presumably part of an early circular *llan* before the churchyard assumed its present rectangular form. The usual interpretation of these circles of yews is that they mark the sites of pre-Christian ceremonial or sacred sites, although quite often the trees are of an age where they could be associated with early saint cells of the sixth and seventh centuries. The largest of the yews at this site – a male tree with a girth of 26 feet 6 inches (8.1 metres) – would seem to fit this timescale since 1,500 years old would be a reasonable estimate of its age. There are musings of a stone circle once having existed at this site, largely inspired by a substantial stone embedded beneath the hollow trunk of one tree, inferring that the yews replaced the stones. Clearly there is a large gap between the oldest yew planting and the establishment of the first church, making any precise attribution for the yews' presence purely speculative.

'...a splendid collection of fine yew trees around the modest church...'

The largest yew, which grows atop a small mound, appears to be a twin-trunked specimen, although evidence around the base suggests that it is the remnant of a much larger tree, perhaps throwing its planting date into an even earlier era. Many old and weathered gravestones lean at odd angles beneath this tree, but one in particular takes the eye. The carving at the head of the nineteenth-century stone clearly depicts a grave beneath the protective bough of an overhanging yew tree – the most sought-after resting place for the deceased in Wales, and perhaps a vestige of pagan superstition that the sacred yew imbues some of its immortality in the soul passing over.

Llanafan Fawr Yew

It is easy to rumble straight through the small settlement of Llanafan Fawr, sitting amid the rolling moorland some five miles to the west of Builth Wells, without pausing to enjoy some of the hidden stories that this unassuming village has to offer.

7 Map D4

Opposite the fifteenth-century Red Lion, with its claim to being the oldest pub in Wales (twelfth-century origins), stands the fine Victorian church of St. Afan. This is just the latest of a long line of churches built on this site since the early medieval period. However, the fact that the church appears to be built on a mound and the original outline of the churchyard was once circular suggests that a pre-Christian origin to the site seems likely. Certainly there has been a settlement here for at least 2,000 years; witness the nearby well-defined mound and ditch with surrounding rampart in a field to the south of the pub. Quite probably coeval with this structure, a magnificent male yew tree stands to the east of the church.

From a distance this is the classic, voluminous domed structure of a healthy open-grown yew. Clamber carefully beneath the enveloping fronds to discover a huge fragmented bole, measuring some 31 feet 10 inches (9.7 metres) at ground level. The tree has long since hollowed and now manifests as three principal trunks with two additional large stems and a stump. Much adventitious growth decks the lower bole.

'...discover a huge fragmented bole, measuring some 31 feet 10 inches (9.7metres) at ground level.'

St. Afan or Avanus, to whom the church is dedicated, was a Welsh saint most probably ascribed to the tenth century and known as Bishop Jeuan. It is said that he had only been made bishop for a single day before he was murdered by marauding Vikings about a mile from where the church now stands. His tomb survives to this day in the churchyard – a huge slab of stone inscribed *hic jacet sanctus avanus episcopus* (here lies St. Afan bishop). Although the stone only dates from the fourteenth century, there are records of the site being an important focus for pilgrims as far back as the thirteenth century.

A much stranger memorial also stands in the churchyard – a gravestone which is unique in Britain that recounts by name both the deceased beneath and the man who murdered him – 'John Price Who Was Murdered On The Darren Hill In This Parish By R. Lewis April 21 1826.' Rees Lewis was eventually caught, sentenced and hung at Brecon.

Right: Church of St. Afan with its ancient yew and a more recently planted Irish yew.

Alltmawr Yew

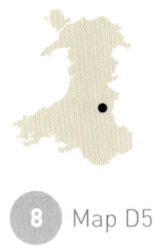

8 Map D5

After consulting various books and the excellent Ancient Yew Group website there didn't seem to be anything wildly exceptional about this yew apart from the fact that it was billed as having a girth of 30 feet (9.14 metres). However, as with so many of these great old trees it's actually the location that can extract something extraordinary out of modest expectations.

Finding the yew at Alltmawr proved challenging to the point of exasperation. Alltmawr is marked on the map as a village on the road down the Wye Valley, a couple of miles south of Builth Wells. However, strangely enough, it doesn't actually feature as a village where it's expected to be; instead a little hamlet called Abernant (which is signed) seems to have stolen the mantle of Alltmawr. Eventually I discovered the narrow, gated lane that leads up the hillside to the tiny church of St. Mauritius – not a saint to whom churches are commonly dedicated in this country, but St. Maurice (the same saint) is often encountered in Europe, particularly France. Apparently he was the leader of the legendary Roman Theban legion in the third century, a legion entirely composed of Christians. What the connection is with Alltmawr I know not. The church is one of the tiniest in Wales, measuring a mere 35 feet long, and originates from the thirteenth century, although much of what is here today is the result of eighteenth and nineteenth-century rebuilding and renovation.

Towering above the church, in the south-west corner of the churchyard, is the splendid single yew tree, with a rather pleasant rustic bench wedged beneath

the great bole for anyone with a moment to stop and contemplate their mortality ... or perhaps immortality if we engage with the spirit of the yew.

The tree appears to be in excellent health, although at some point a large chunk must have broken away from the south side. This may explain the hugely varying girth measurements that are recorded – 30 feet (9.1 metres) would include the base of the tree where the loss occurred, but the lesser figure of 24 feet (7.3 metres) probably excludes this. The larger dimension would surely suggest a more realistic vintage for the tree.

What makes this whole site worth a visit is the dramatic contrast between tree and church. The diminutive little structure appears totally dwarfed by the billowing dark canopy and looming, or perhaps protective, form of the mighty yew; clearly estalished in its rightful place long before those new-fangled Christian folk set up down below.

Llanthony Whitebeams

9 Map D5

By their very nature many whitebeams grow in physically challenging locations, principally where nothing can disturb them – whether it be human intervention or the questing jaws of sheep and deer. Llanthony Whitebeam (*Sorbus stenophylla*), which is almost completely confined to the Vale of Ewyas, south of Hay-on-Wye, is no exception.

This is a marvellously secluded valley set in the Black Mountains, and known principally for the romantic ruins of the twelfth-century Llanthony Priory and

'...marvellously secluded valley set in the Black Mountains...'

the tiny church at Capel-y-ffin, set around with its circle of ancient yew trees, which surely make this a pre-Christian sacred site. To the east, the route of Offa's Dyke traces the ridge of Black Hill, recently made famous by the evocative book 'On the Black Hill' by Bruce Chatwin.

For hundreds if not thousands of years whitebeams had been growing high above this valley, unremarked as anything of unusual interest, until they attracted the attention of Victorian botanist Rev. Augustin Ley (see also Ley's Whitebeam p.124) in 1874. He realised that they were of a slightly different form to other whitebeams, but he probably considered them some sort of anomaly rather than a new species. In fact it wasn't until the 1950s that the trees were included under the banner of *Sorbus porrigentiformis*, but more recent

Above: Vale of Ewyas, looking towards Gospel Pass. The whitebeams may be found on the crags of Darren Lwyd, on the far left of this view.

scientific studies of the trees' genetic profile by Proctor and Groenhof in 1992 established a link to *Sorbus cambrensis* (see also Welsh whitebeam p.70). However, largely due to a quite definite and different leaf shape, which is more narrowly cuneate (tapering towards the leaf base) and with more deeply incised teeth than Welsh whitebeam, it was deemed by Rich and Proctor in 2009 to be a new species. These exacting criteria show how specific the identification and description of a new species can be, and beyond the comprehension of the layman botanist. Around 200 specimens of this tree are currently known in the valley.

Again, extreme caution must be exercised when setting out to find these trees as they grow in precipitous locations. Travelling south from Hay-on-Wye the single track road leads enticingly across the moorland below Hay Bluff, over the Gospel Pass and down into the Vale of Ewyas. All is wild; all is remote. The scattered farms and barns, some inhabited, many derelict, dot the rugged landscape as they have for centuries. This is sheep country, but also, here and there, wild ponies roam the fells, their shaggy unkempt manes and tails blown like tattered banners in the stiff breeze. There are few walls or fences in the upper reaches of the valley, so it's easy to strike off for the top. The crags of Darren Lwyd may only host seven specimens, but the view from the top is breathtaking and worth every step of the climb. A little to the west yet more trees can be seen on Tarren yr Esgob (more than 50 trees grow here), and since these sites only harbour this species there is no possibility of confusion with other whitebeams.

Llanvihangel Court
Sweet Chestnuts

10 Map D5

South of the A465, near the village of Llanvihangel Crucorney, lies the remnants of a once spectacular avenue of sweet chestnuts (*Castanea sativa*), with unusual if unsubstantiated origins. This is the ghost of a grand approach to the sixteenth-century mansion of Llanvihangel Court, now cut off from the big house, sold off many years ago and forgotten for decades. The remaining trees are hanging on to life by a thread.

Above & pages 52–53:
The remnants of the once grand southern avenue of sweet chestnuts leading to Llanvihangel Court.

'...the trees have been known for a long time as the Armada Avenue.'

A conversation with the farmer who currently owns the land where this amazing historic feature survives reveals that the trees have been known for a long time as the Armada Avenue. The long-held local belief is that these trees were planted after the British defeat of the Spanish Armada in 1588, using chestnuts that were plundered from the stricken and captured vessels.

It is a great story, but could there be any substance to the claim? It is very likely that sweet or Spanish chestnuts were on board the ships, as they were a staple food, but with the options of gold, silver, weaponry, and probably strong drink on hand for the looters, one wonders why on earth anyone would pocket some chestnuts. This is also a tradition that persists with the chestnut avenues at Croft Castle in Herefordshire.

Today there are roughly 50 trees left, showing various levels of vitality. Some have died completely, their bleached carcasses laid low or looming large with wild corkscrew limbs. Others show much sign of decline and decay, while a few seem to have shrugged off all attempts by disease, time and the elements to level them. It seems likely that a water-borne disease called phytopthora has hastened the demise of some trees. Clearly the effects of barking and compaction from livestock also make life a little harder for some trees too, but this could be remedied. The enormous size of the biggest trees, with 26 to 30 feet (7.9 to 9.1 metres) girths does lend credence to their age being around 400–450 years old and thus dropping them conveniently into the timeframe for the Armada story.

Above: Lanvihangel Court 1680.

It was while talking with a local resident that I discovered the existence of a painting from 1680 that depicted Llanvihangel Court with its surrounding landscape and, what turned out to be most fascinating, various avenues of trees approaching the house. The view is painted from the north, and seems to show a double avenue – broadleaf trees on the inner one and pines on the outer one – running up to the northern, front façade of the house. Pines also form another avenue through the park from the north-east and in a line around the park perimeter. Scots pines certainly existed here until the mid-twentieth century; another popular tradition being that these trees signified safe harbour for Jacobite sympathizers in the wake of the uprising of 1745, although clearly these trees would have been planted long before this association transpired. The present owner has recently replanted a pine avenue here. There is what might be a clump of cedars in view to the east of the northern avenue (their size making them a very early planting), as well as extensive orchards to the west of the house; both of these features are now long gone. However, beyond the house another avenue of broadleaf trees may be seen, making an approach from the south. In the painting they are small in scale, but upon closer inspection they were already fairly substantial trees – without doubt the chestnut avenue that survives today.

The painting is naïve in style, typical of the period, where the unknown artist has implicated several of the local landmarks but all completely out of scale. Skirrid, the distant Blorenge, the River Monnow and the dome of Sugar Loaf all appear in a hugely compromised distillation of these features. No doubt it pleased John Arnold, the owner of Llanvihangel Court at that time, who must have commissioned it. Early estate paintings such as this are exceptionally rare and it is a thrill to see the house with its attendant parkland, avenues and trees from 330 years ago, even allowing for a degree of artistic licence.

Millennium Derwen

11 Map E5

There is no shortage of impressive oak trees in Wales, and the border counties in particular are home to several massive specimens. Girths of 20 to 24 feet (6.1 to 7.3 metres) will always present magnificent looking trees which will have estimated ages of between 300 and 500 years. Oaks in excess of 30 feet (9.1 metres) in girth are altogether exceptional and must be estimated in age ranges beyond 700 years; although the older these trees become the smaller their annual growth increments will be. The fact that almost all of these ancient oaks are hollow by the time they reach such great age means that there is little chance of truly establishing their exact vintage.

With this in mind, discovering a tree such as the Great Welsh Oak, with a girth of 32 feet 6 inches (9.9 metres), quietly living out its dotage in a field near Llantilio Crossenny, is a fantastic glimpse of a tree that has probably taken at least 800 years to grow into the craggy old bystander amid the commercial orchards of a farm growing cider apples. Judging by the relatively small amount of live branches on this oak it is probably approaching the end of its allotted span, but while it lives it has been recorded as the fifth largest oak in the whole of Wales.

Nobody can know why it has survived so long, although pollarding has clearly helped in the distant past, or whether it once had a role to play, such as a boundary marker, but in 2000 local folk decided to honour the tree with a

special appellation. It is now known as the Millennium Derwen (*derwen* being Welsh for oak), and by naming the tree this would seem to be an excellent way of putting it on the national map of famous and notable Welsh trees, ensuring that, for the last few years of its life at least, it receives the care, respect and admiring visitations that such ancient trees deserve.

'...a fantastic glimpse of a tree that has probably taken at least 800 years to grow into the craggy old bystander...'

Crickhowell Black Poplars

12 Map D5

The native black poplar (*Populus nigra* subsp. *betulifolia*) is a tree that finds its natural place either along the banks of watercourses or in the hedgerows and meadows of floodplains. With the latter habitat now seriously threatened by ongoing agricultural drainage schemes, some of the last refuges for this scarce native broadleaf are riverbanks and streamsides. However, many other poplars, principally grey poplar and the hybrid black poplar, also haunt these riverine habitats, so that distinguishing the native black poplar from its cousins can sometimes be difficult. Also, when all these poplars thrive in close confines to one another the genetic integrity of each species is often compromised since the trees hybridise so readily.

On the banks of the River Usk, on the Glanusk Estate, hard by the old stone river bridge built in 1706 to cross into Crickhowell, stand two of the finest and most instantly recognisable native black poplars in the land. Until a few years ago there were three trees here, but one succumbed to gales and crashed to the ground, fortunately not taking its brethren with it. The surviving trees are two of the largest in Britain and it is to be hoped that they will remain as a distinctive landmark for many years to come.

'...two of the finest and most instantly recognisable native black poplars in the land.'

Following the course of the River Usk southwards several other black poplars come into view along the riverbanks. Since the male/female imbalance usually precludes reproduction via seed, this begs the question as to how some of these trees might have sprung up. Quite often boughs or twigs are blown from trees or snapped off by floods. These float down river and may embed themselves in the soft earth of the banks, easily taking root and creating new trees, showing that even in adversity this remarkable tree has the capacity to reproduce.

The Weird Birches of Ty-uchaf

These birch trees have no given title, and grow unheeded in old upland pastures above the Usk Valley. They have not been celebrated in any way due to historical or cultural connections and even the farmer who owns them was surprised that they were of particular interest.

Birch has traditionally been a tree of little account in Britain. A great coloniser; its massive showers of tiny, winged seeds blow far and wide, insinuating themselves into the slightest crack or hollow to gradually cover any open space they can get. Regarded by foresters as weeds they seem to have little

13 Map D5

commercial value other than performing sheltering roles to other emerging broadleaf trees. The true grace and beauty of an open-grown birch tree is something special to behold, although they seldom live to any great age, 80–100 years being quite exceptional. In the depths of some of the old Caledonian forests great rugged trees have been noted which could easily be well in excess of a 100 years old, but south of the border such trees are rare.

'Clad in mosses and lichens, thriving in this pure upland air, they writhe from their rocky plinths...'

Searching for a remarkable ash tree (see Ty-uchaf Wall Ash p.64) took me high on the hills near Llanelly, on the south side of the Usk Valley, but before I could track down the ash I stumbled upon these two enormous downy birches (*Betula pubescans*) growing among the dilapidated remains of old dry stone walls – old field boundaries long abandoned. Photographing them from every angle produced an endless array of weird and wonderful images. Clad in mosses and lichens, thriving in this pure upland air, they writhe from their

rocky plinths, posing questions as to their survival. Why have they never been cut back for fuel? Exactly how old are they? One tree bears a semblance of having once been laid in a vain attempt to make a hedge, but has then simply been left to grow up again unhindered. The larger of this tree's two boles has a girth of almost 14 feet (4.2 metres) – exceptional for birch. The other tree, straddling the tumbled wall, has grown up as five separate boles from its convoluted root mass, each one dividing again and criss-crossing with one another. It is hard to believe that these trees can be less than 100 years old and, in this upland location, where trees tend to grow a lot slower, it's possible to think that they may even be 200 years old.

To my knowledge nobody has recognised the significance of these two birches until now, so it is refreshing to get this neglected species a bit of the limelight at long last.

Ty-uchaf Wall Ash

14 Map D5

High on the hills, up above the Usk Valley there would seem to be many strange and unaccounted trees quietly growing in old woods and pastures as well as clinging to the precipitous limestone crags, but then this landscape lends itself to such forgotten trees. Narrow, deep-cut lanes, many centuries old, twist and turn up the hillsides with bends so sharp that one can barely scrape a car around them. Once there was mining and quarrying up here, but now it is given over to hill farmers and folk who just crave a peaceful retreat.

Old drovers' roads and green lanes mark the ancient thoroughfares up here and alongside them run drystone walls, now frequently tumbled and neglected as well as hedgerows with massively outgrown trees which were once trimmed and laid. This ash tree (*Fraxinus excelsior*) is one of those that was once laid or pleached into a hedgerow, but surely well over a century ago.

Ash is a tree that responds extremely well to regular cutting, and up in these remote parts they would have been regularly cut over for fuel wood; the best firewood available as it burns green or seasoned. The massive lateral boughs of this tree stretch out along the top of the wall creating the impression that this was once a wall with a hedge right next to it or even above it.

'...a strange, awesome and unique tree...'

The substantial old bole is firmly wedged amongst the big boulders of the wall, so that the whole tree is well propped and braced. A rough measurement of the tree from end to end was around 25 feet (7.6 metres). A tree that has grown this way, shaped by human hand, is very difficult to age, but could easily be 150–200 years old. Its mode of growth has made it into a strange, awesome and unique tree, surely more than enough to wriggle its way into the pages of this book.

Least or Lesser Whitebeam

15 Map D5

Some of the most exciting places to find rare or unusual trees are often the most dangerous and difficult to get to. The north-east edge of Mynydd Llangatwg, high above the Usk Valley, where the hills plunge suddenly away as the limestone cliffs of Craig y Cilau, bears perfect testimony to this assertion. So often where there is limestone there has been quarrying, and in the not too distant past it was a vital element of the local economy here. Happily (for the trees at least) this has all ceased.

Viewed from the distant market town of Crickhowell in the valley bottom, these cliffs might support vegetation much like any of the other similar features in the landscape hereabouts. So it must have been a happy discovery for the Victorian and Edwardian botanists who began exploring these hillsides when they found a wealth of plants and trees, some of which seemed ever so slightly different to the species with which they were already familiar.

Seven members of the *Sorbus* genus occur with some frequency at Craig y Cilau. However, it was botanist Augustin Ley who first realised that certain small leaved whitebeams here were not exactly like many others he had recorded elsewhere. The leaves were noticeably smaller and with a distinctive lobed profile. In 1893 (12 June to be exact – like most keen naturalists he kept a detailed diary), Ley found what he dubbed *Pyrus minima* (the Victorians tended to lump the rowans and whitebeams in with the pears), which would later become known as *Sorbus minima*. It is thought that lesser or least whitebeam, as it has become commonly known, could be a hybrid of rock whitebeam (*Sorbus rupicola*) and rowan (*Sorbus aucuparia*) – in much the same way as Ley's whitebeam, but simply taking a slightly different form. As it transpired this particular tree only grew at four specific sites, all within a few miles of each other. Sadly, one of these was subsequently lost due to extensive quarrying, so now there are just three sites where it grows. Recent surveys have identified at least 780 trees from these sites, but bear in mind this is the world population of the species. When you see the precipitous nature of the terrain upon which these trees grow the difficulty of achieving accurate surveys becomes obvious.

A walk along the cliff top at Craig y Cilau is a bracing experience indeed, and worth it for the stunning views alone. Here you can see for miles either way

Lesser whitebeam clings to the cliff edge on Craig y Cilau, above the Usk Valley. Sugar Loaf mountain in the distance.

along the Usk Valley and, to the east, the rugged hummocks of the Black Mountains stretch away towards Herefordshire. The limestone crags are a 'time-trap' where trees and plants have regenerated, multiplied and hybridised quietly for thousands of years. Large-leaved lime, a scarce native, has grown here for thousands of years, as pollen records from the bog beneath the crags attest. Rowan is here in some order, as well as much ash and hawthorn (*Crataegus Monogyna*). Where the hawthorns are accessible to sheep and rabbits, or have been whipped by the wind, they have been moulded into tiny bonsai versions of themselves. Up on the very top of the crags, where a narrow path demands the utmost caution, the rare and beautiful whitebeams grow out across the void from the tightest and apparently most barren nooks and crannies. One can only marvel at their tenacity. There are three other whitebeams here, the rarest of which is narrow-leaved whitebeam (*Sorbus leptophylla*), with only 74 trees identified between two sites; again, this is the world population.

'...the rare and beautiful whitebeams grow out across the void from the tightest and apparently most barren nooks and crannies.'

Below: Lesser whitebeam flourishes along the cliff tops in this view eastwards along Craig y Cilau, with the town of Crickhowell and Sugar Loaf mountain in the distance.

Welsh Whitebeam

16 Map D5

For a tree boldly introduced with such a grand, national epithet it might, understandably, be assumed that this is a tree of widespread distribution in its native land. Not so, for the tree only appears within a very localised area just to the east of Brynmawr, where the throb of traffic roaring along the Heads of the Valleys road runs down into the Usk Valley, through Cwm Clydach. The limestone cliffs on either side of the road typify the sort of habitat where the whitebeam tribe usually thrives.

Head off the main road and seek a narrow country lane, just to the north, following the contours below Darren Disgwylfa until an old quarry is encountered on the west side of the road – this is Pantydarren. Huge limestone slabs tower above the road; a lush rock garden to the trees and plants which find purchase in every nook and cranny. This is perhaps the easiest of locations to pin down the Welsh whitebeam (*Sorbus cambrensis*), for no other whitebeams grow at this site to confuse identification, and to the untutored eye this tree could easily be confused with common whitebeam (*Sorbus aria*) – a tree endemic across the whole of Britain. However Welsh whitebeams only number around 100–150 specimens, and are mostly specific to the crags around the eastern slopes of Mynydd Llangatwg, with a few more trees to be found a little further up the Usk Valley at Craig y Cilau. Welsh whitebeam was first distinguished from the more widespread *Sorbus porrigentiformis* during investigations by Proctor and Groenhof in 1992, but not named as a separate species until 2009 by Rich and Proctor.

The view out across the Usk Valley from Pantydarren is spectacular, but it must be said that there is a rather sad issue of some people having decided to use the old quarry here as a dumping ground for rubbish and a suitable location for torching cars. Fortunately, the whitebeams are able to rise above this, set high up on the crags as most of them are. Caution must be exercised if you want to get a closer look at these trees as they are quite precariously situated – the main reason that they have survived so well, out of the reach of hungry sheep which find them most tasty. Some of the trees here are quite large and there is ample evidence of coppicing in the distant past, although whether this was purposeful harvesting by man or natural occurrences due to extreme weather is uncertain.

Below: Welsh whitebeam on crags at Darren Disgwylfa near Llanelly.

Ty Mawr Oak

17 Map D6

I recently had an opportunity to visit a private estate south of Abergavenny, after a recommendation from a friend that, 'these people really do have some stunning trees,' which was all I needed to lift the phone and arrange a date. I was given the grand tour of the garden, introduced to many wonderful exotics and cultivars, as well as the mighty Oriental plane that dominates the drive, before being given a swift tour of the estate to enjoy many other remarkable trees and tracts of woodland.

Finally, we swung into a large open pasture, where one of the most beautiful oaks I have seen commanded the view. With an impressive, but not unduly vast girth of 24 feet (7.3 metres) there will be a handful of other oaks perhaps as old or as big as this tree elsewhere in Wales, yet it is still more than worthy of joining the ranks of other heritage trees within these pages, The owners had searched family history and local archives in the hope that some historic connection or reference might lead to a fitting name for this great old oak, but absolutely nothing could be discovered. The tree has now been dubbed the Ty Mawr Oak by the family in deference to the nearby farmhouse – the name Ty Mawr means the big house. Somehow the very act of naming a tree feels as if it puts it more firmly on the map, makes it part of the family or community, a tangible thing to look after, and begins to create its own story for the future.

The tree's form is impressive, for it throws up three vast boughs from its burry base, but from only 3 or 4 feet above the ground. If this union was higher then the natural assumption would be that it was an old pollard, but it appears more likely to be a maiden, thus making its size and longevity even more remarkable.

Closer examination reveals that an aerial holly tree has been developing from a crevice in one bough and there is also the fairly unusual occurrence of a couple of little clumps of wall pennywort or navelwort finding purchase in some other little hollows in the bark. A slight worry for the tree might be the continued trampling of cattle around the base, perhaps leading to some root compaction in the future, but at present the tree appears to be in the pink.

'The tree's form is impressive, for it throws up three vast boughs from its burry base, but from only 3 or 4 feet above the ground.'

The Blorenge Beeches

18 Map D6

To the west of Abergavenny in the Usk Valley, hunched high above the town, sits The Blorenge, an 1,800 feet (548 metres) hill beyond which the once industrious coal rich valleys of Wales run one after another. From the mid-nineteenth century coal from the valleys fed the iron industry of south Wales, but prior to that it was charcoal that fired the furnaces. This meant that coppice wood for charcoal making was required in some order, and the oak and beech woods of The Blorenge were ideally situated to fulfil this need. A network of ancient trackways and paths weaves across the hillsides, and there is still evidence of an old rackway which, more than 200 years ago, lowered coal from the mines on the plateau down into the valley, returning up the hill with pit props for the mine tunnels.

'These mega beeches are so awesome simply because they have been neglected...'

Left: View down into The Punchbowl through one of the old beech pollards.
Below: A long neglected beech hedge still shows signs of having once been laid.

Nestled, almost hidden away, on the upper slopes lies The Punchbowl a dramatic feature that appears as if someone has taken a giant scoop out of the hillside and left this wonderful hemispherical depression. It is thought that it may well be a glacial cirque, where snow and ice eroded the sandstone about a million years ago. At the bottom of the hollow lies a small pond, but this has been formed in recent times by damming to stop the naturally occurring marshy ground from draining away. From the Middle Ages onwards the Blorenge would have been managed as wood-pasture common, which seems to be confirmed by the presence of many massive old pollard beeches (*Fagus sylvatica*). There are ashes here too, but it's the beeches that steal the show. The Woodland Trust has owned The Punchbowl for the last twenty-five years and there may soon come a time when the ongoing management of the great beeches will pose a problem: to pollard or not to pollard?

These mega beeches are so awesome simply because they have been neglected and become vastly outgrown since nobody has needed their wood for several generations, although with the current upsurge in demand for wood-fuel they may become part of the commercial equation once again. If they do remain uncut there will come a time when the trees will either go into natural decline or fall victim to storm damage. Equally, if they are hacked back too dramatically they could be traumatised and die anyway. It's a tough call, as they are all such magnificent and individual trees. The Woodland Trust is busily planting seed from these trees to maintain the genetic strain, which is obviously well adapted to conditions on The Blorenge.

Several ancient tracks and holloways lead up the hill from Coed-y-person on to the hill, or down from the narrow hilltop lane to Blaenavon into The Punchbowl, many lined with huge, overhanging beeches, the silver-grey coils and buttresses of their roots locked around boulders or clutching at thin air – a Tolkienesque experience if ever there was one. Some are pollards, some coppice stools and some simply the untended remnants of long outgrown hedges – their vaguely horizontal lower limbs a distant memory of a once finely laid hedge.

Right: Early morning view from The Blorenge. Beeches in the foreground with Skirrid Fawr beyond.

Many of these trees must be descended from naturally occurring trees, for this remarkable place is one of only a handful of sites in south-east Wales where beech is thought to have colonised naturally after the last Ice Age. Beech throughout the rest of Wales is considered naturalized, but from introduced origins.

Llangattock-juxta-Usk Yew

19 Map D6

The majority of yew trees featured in this book are here largely because of their extreme size and great antiquity, and yet yews do have the capacity to grow in some very unusual places and, in so doing, often manifest themselves in unique and particularly strange forms. One such tree is a male yew on the edge of St. Cadoc's churchyard in the tiny hamlet of Llangattock-juxta-Usk, confusingly also marked on the Ordnance Survey maps as The Bryn, which lies about three miles south-east of Abergavenny on a bend in the River Usk.

'...a tree that appears to be attempting to tiptoe away from the scene on several 'legs'.

The church stands only a few yards away from the main railway line between Hereford and Newport and has several handsome yews growing around it, the most remarkable of all concealing its strange mode of growth until you step outside the confines of the churchyard and into the adjacent field. A gap in the perimeter stone wall creates a perfect framework for a tree that appears to be attempting to tiptoe away from the scene on several 'legs'. Quite how this part of the lower bole has grown like this is a mystery, but perhaps there was once an earth bank here, for it has the appearance of once having been more of a root system rather than a trunk. The tree has been measured at about 24 feet (7.3 metres) around, above these 'legs'.

A strange tale from the nineteenth century, gleaned from the transactions of the Llancarfan Society, attends the church. Apparently, John Upton, a local builder, stole three of the four bells from the belfry. He later fled his creditors, joined the Russian army and fought in the Crimean War. The local belief is that he took the bells to Sebastopol. One assumes that the reason for his misdemeanour was that he intended to sell the bells, but exactly why they accompanied him to the Crimea is a mystery. It would be marvellous to relate a story about the weird yew, but sadly there are no accounts. However, for those with an enquiring mind, a bizarre yet beautiful contemporary diversion attends the tree at www.treegirl.org

Bettws Newydd Yew

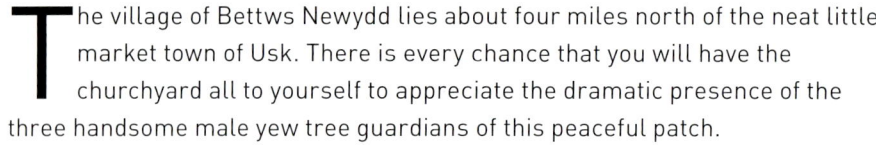

'This ancient, bleached, death-mask apparition of a tree conceals an inner secret of enduring and renewable life.'

Above: Sculpture in the church porch, made from a fallen fragment of the Bettws Newydd Yew.

The village of Bettws Newydd lies about four miles north of the neat little market town of Usk. There is every chance that you will have the churchyard all to yourself to appreciate the dramatic presence of the three handsome male yew tree guardians of this peaceful patch.

The largest of the three trees stands hard by the footpath, a massive specimen with a girth of 33 feet (10.1 metres) placing it firmly amongst the largest and oldest yews in Wales. This ancient, bleached, death-mask apparition of a tree conceals an inner secret of enduring and renewable life. The darker coloured bole visible within the old shell is actually a new generation of the tree derived from an aerial root, which has grown down from the inside of the declining original tree, found purchase within the rich mulch of decaying matter in the base, and then forged a new presence to carry the tree forward for a few more centuries. The inner tree was already well established by 1876 and today measures 7 feet 6 inches (2.3 metres) in girth. All ancient yews have strange, singular appearances, but this tree is probably one of the most striking in the whole of Wales.

Elsewhere in the churchyard are two somewhat smaller yews, each one a unique character. In the porch of the church a piece of yew timber, fallen from the great tree, has been lovingly carved and inscribed by a local artist – a memorial to the affection held by the local populace for their mighty yew tree.

Monmouthshire Orchards

21 Map E6

Frederick apple

C ast an eye through any written work on the subject of orchards and fruit varieties and you will be hard pressed to discover very much information about this branch of arboriculture in Wales. Just across the border, in Herefordshire, records are plentiful on all aspects of orcharding. Several fine pomonas over the last 200 years meticulously record scores of apples and pears for dessert, culinary and vintage (cider and perry) purposes with treatises detailing their respective qualities, as well as preferred methods of cultivation. Seek a clue to an unknown apple variety today and all the reference material is there to assist you. Travel back across the border into Monmouthshire and there are no written records concerning the long orcharding tradition, and no reference works for identifying varieties of Welsh origin, something which also applies to the whole of Wales.

General knowledge of orchard culture in Britain usually comes from the early tomes on farming and land management, and it is known that substantial orchards were established in Monmouthshire, as well as Brecon and Radnor, from the end of the seventeenth century onwards. As with the rest of Britain, there is every likelihood that the monastic gardens of Wales as far back as the medieval period were akin to the modern trial orchards of today. The monks were great gardeners and experimenters, undoubtedly well acquainted with the art of grafting to promote the best varieties, and thus laying the foundations for the farmers in the uncloistered world to carry this knowledge forward with their own orchards.

The vast majority of orchards in the county today are remnants of what must have been extensive and highly productive fruit farms. Dessert and culinary fruit were usually sent to market, while vintage fruit was often reserved for making the cider and perry consumed by the farmer, his family and the farm workers. The whole cider-making cycle, including planting trees, grafting (which was usually on to crab stocks), pruning, gathering the fruit, processing and pressing the pulp, and enjoying the product was simply a welcome element of the seasonal round on the farm.

Above: This wonderful old apple orchard with its big, rambling standard trees was photographed at Twyn-y-Sheriff in 1996. Today, the lower barns have become a house, a drive has swept through the orchard, and only one solitary tree remains. The world moves on and changes happen, but the thought of losing all our old orchards in this way is deeply worrying.

Right: Breakwell's Seedling.

Remnant orchards are sometimes found as small patches of ground, almost like an addition to a farm's kitchen garden, where anything and everything would have been grown to supplement the family's diet including plums, pears, cherries, dessert and culinary apples, as well as walnuts. Orchards which occupy larger pieces of ground were where the commercial crops of cider apples and perry pears would have been grown, as many farms were already supplying the larger cider and perry making companies by the end of the nineteenth century. Still, orchards were usually quite close to the farm buildings or roads to minimise the distance that the fruit had to be carried for milling or for carting away. Livestock were frequently grazed beneath the trees and in some orchards, with wide spaced rows of trees, the land was tilled and crops planted. Many of these large orchards are today often almost completely bereft of trees, and what is left has usually been neglected simply because nobody has a use for the fruit any more.

Above: Hillside perry pear grove, Court Farm, Llanvihangel-Ystern-Llewern.
Top right: Just two of the ten different yet unknown varieties of perry pears discovered at Court Farm.

At the outset of working on this book I found information on old orchards in Monmouthshire difficult to acquire, so I set out one morning in mid-April to see if I could find anything of interest for myself. Working on the principle that the pear trees were now in flower I thought I should be able to spot them in the landscape without too much trouble. I drove for many miles through the tract of Monmouthshire bordered by Abergavenny, Raglan and Monmouth, tracking down several individual pear trees, some of which appeared to be seedlings or wildings in hedgerows, and the odd group of two or three decrepit trees in the corners of fields. However, when in flower it is difficult to know whether these are dessert pears or perry pears. It took all morning before I spied a large farm orchard with anything like a substantial collection of trees.

Court Farm, at Llanvihangel-Ystern-Llewern, has been owned by the Baker family for the last 50 years, and they were more than happy for me to while away an hour or so in what remains of their old orchard. The large field, which was then also being used as nursery grazing for ewes with their newborn lambs, contains about 15 pear trees and a handful of apple trees. The shapes of pear trees are often very specific to individual varieties – some are low and spreading while others, most typically perry pears, are tall, very upright forms, usually with decidedly arching boughs. The experience of photographing the orchard was a mixture of emotions. Sadness at the decrepit state of so many of the trees (several of which were just dead hulks laid low), but equally of wonder at the rugged old trees still soldiering on, some of which could be well in excess of 100 years old. I tried to imagine what this orchard must have looked like in its prime, full of well-tended and productive trees when the farm was actively making its own perry, something that hasn't occurred here for a very long time.

Above: Dessert pear trees

Top right: A massive perry pear tree in a hedgerow
at Llanvihangel-Ystern-Llewern – around 50 feet
high and with a girth of 9 feet (2.7 metres) this must
surely be in excess of 200 years old.

Above: A typical remnant orchard at Lydart with a scattering of mainly unidentified varieties, although the tree in the foreground is a Breakwell's Seedling. Trees are festooned with mistletoe and the numerous hollows provide excellent habitat for bats and nesting birds.

I wondered what varieties might be in the orchard. Were they traditional Monmouthshire or Welsh varieties, or perhaps ones shipped in from Herefordshire or Gloucestershire? Were they rare, possibly unique, varieties that may only exist in this village, or even just on this one farm? I dreamt of a conservation orchard with all the known Monmouthshire varieties archived and flourishing for posterity ... little knowing at the time that there is such a thing. I asked the family if they knew much about the pears, but beyond the rather tasty dessert pears on a couple of the trees there was no knowledge. Just before I left they pointed to another orchard on a hill above a neighbouring farm (which they also own) and suggested I take a look.

Half an hour later I was sitting beneath a grove of about 10 pear trees which runs up a small hollow in the hillside high above the farm, where they have probably long been protected from the worst of the elements. Unlike the other orchard this group of trees was some distance from its farm, but at least it would have been downhill all the way to the press. An unusual feature of these trees was the complete lack of any evidence of graft scars, indicating that they were very likely planted as seedlings. In the hedge below this group stands one of the largest pear trees that I have ever seen, probably in excess of 50 feet high, and a trunk with a girth of 9 feet (2.7 metres), making this tree almost certainly in excess of 200 years old. I vowed to return to both these sites in the autumn.

As the fruit began to ripen I did return and, as usual, gleaned more knowledge of the trees I had only before seen in flower. It transpired that three of the trees whose shape had convinced me that they must be perry pears actually bore rather handsome, large green dessert pears. Plucked from the tree as hard as rocks, after 10 days on my kitchen table they were nothing short of luscious. Conversely, a large, low-spreading tree, with a girth of over 8 feet (2.4 metres), which I assumed could not be a perry pear, again proved me wrong. In the hillside orchard, where I had conjectured in the spring about the seedling trees, I felt vindicated by the fact that no two trees were the same variety – a most unusual occurrence in a large group of fruit trees. Between the two orchards I discovered 10 quite different varieties of perry pear. The journey continues as, with the help of local experts, I struggle to find out what they are.

It is interesting to note that between 1908 and 1918 the National Fruit and Cider Institute (formed in 1904) was responsible for planting five trial orchards of perry pears in Monmouthshire, one of which, at Hendre Home Farm, was barely a couple of miles across the fields from Court Farm. The varieties planted there were from Gloucestershire, and none of these seem to tally with the Court Farm varieties. In fact, sadly, all five of these trial orchards have been grubbed out, although a 1962 photograph of Hendre Home Farm orchard shows it to have been a splendid sight.

Below: Monmouthshire Burgundy perry pears at Raglan Parc Golf Club.

Wishing to spread my net wider, I contacted Dave Matthews of the Welsh Perry and Cider Society to see what he knew about Monmouthshire apples and pears. Remarkably, it seems as if they are having to glean most of their knowledge through oral traditions handed down from a few of the old farmers who once had productive orchards and made their own farmhouse ciders and perries. Several interviews with these old-timers on the society website prove a fascinating account of an almost forgotten way of life. Dave rues the fact that there is simply no archive information on which to build the story of Monmouthshire's fruit, so with a desire to remedy matters the society is building its own new pomona. A handful of varieties do have a known history. Apples such as Breakwell's Seedling, an early bitter-sharp, was discovered growing near the pigsty at Perthyre Farm in the 1890s and propagated by George Breakwell. Perthyre Farm's very own bitter-sweet Perthyre apple (also known locally as pig's snout or sheep's snout) became widely grown from the 1920s; and Frederick, a full sharp apple which arose in the Forest of Dean in the nineteenth century, but became plentiful in Monmouthshire, are all well known varieties, but where to start with all the unknowns? In the traditional

This bizarre tree, resembling a giant chicken, is a perry pear of the Monmouthshire Burgundy variety, and stands above the 18th green at Raglan Parc Golf Club. Obviously once a farm, it is remarkable that quite a few of these big perry pears have survived the transition – in fact the proprietors of the club are extremely proud of them.

manner Dave and his colleagues arrive at names based on the farm or village where the fruit grows if very site specific (e.g. Berllanderi Green and Red – both from the farm of the same name), or the characteristics of the fruit when more widespread (e.g. Monmouthshire Burgundy). They have also set up what they call their Museum Orchard, pre-empting my own daydream, to preserve two examples of each Welsh variety, and provide a source for grafting material, for future cultivation.

Not every orchard in Monmouthshire is a relict. There are several examples of modern orchards, many of which were originally planted to contract supply the cider giant Bulmers. An interesting example of this is Ty Gwyn, near Skenfrith in the Monnow Valley; originally planted up in 1969 by James McConnel, there is an extensive acreage of cider apples growing on terraces – a most unusual sight. All went smoothly until 2006 when Bulmers were unable to contract the entire tonnage. With the knowledge that several other small craft cider makers were doing rather well, Ty Gwyn embarked upon its own range of ciders, which have been so well received that they haven't looked back. In fact, out of almost 30 small cider producers throughout Wales 11 of them are located in Monmouthshire, creating something of an optimistic outlook for the orcharding renaissance in the county.

Outside the realms of vintage fruit little is known of the various dessert and culinary varieties indigenous to Monmouthshire, although one, a dessert apple called St. Cecilia, is recorded as being raised by John Basham & Sons at Bassaleg in 1900. It was actually a seedling grown from a Cox's Orange Pippin. Described in Joan Morgan and Alison Mitchell's *The New Book of Apples* as, 'Intense, rich, aromatic. Sweet, juicy, crisp, but can be less exciting; rather tough skin.' Still, this was good enough to win the apple a First Class Certificate at the 1919 RHS Show. It would be interesting to know whether any of these still grow in the county.

Growing cider and perry fruit is far more likely to be a profitable venture these days, with the edible apple market flooded by the vast quantities of a few, mainly quite dull varieties imported cheaply from the other side of the world. Every year we risk losing more varieties with their genetic diversity, and more of the old traditional orchards in which they grow; and with these losses go the landscape heritage and regional character, the associated wildlife, the ancient greensward and the flowers. This is why we need people to restore orchards, plant new orchards, and find ways to make them financially viable, thus ensuring we have orchards to pass on to future generations.

Charley Trees

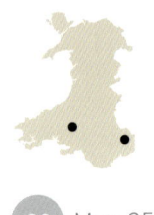

22 Map C5 / E6

Travelling across the Welsh borders a landmark feature that crops up time and time again is a small clump of Scots pines, usually on elevated ground or around old habitations. These are not naturally occurring trees. They are quite definite plantings, but their origins and purpose are blurred in the mists of time.

Scots pine (*Pinus sylvestris*) has not been a true native tree in Wales for several thousand years – the most recent evidence having been derived from pine charcoal discovered in 1930 in a cairn on Anglesey which dates back to about 1500 BC. So the provenance of the pines to be found in Wales today is a moot point. The characteristics of some of the older, larger trees, with their prominent ruddy-coloured platelets of bark and the slightly bluish-green needles seems instantly redolent of the true native subspecies *scotica* which today is only indigenous in the north of Scotland. Could seed have been brought from Scotland? From the second half of the eighteenth century there were an inordinate number of Scottish foresters and estate managers working on the big Welsh estates. Might they have brought seed from home? Whatever the answer, it is a fact that around this time there was a significant upsurge in the planting of pines, both for ornamental reasons and their commercial potential.

A few of the biggest trees growing in these clumps could feasibly be 200 years old or even a little more, although often these stands are multi-generational, probably due to the tree's prodigious self-seeding ability rather than any formal replanting regime. Various traditions attend these clumps, which are often referred to as 'Charley Trees'; namely, that they were planted to commemorate the Jacobite rebellion of 1745, and that wherever they stood the landowner offered safe haven and succour to Jacobite sympathisers. There may be some substance to this since H.A. Hyde in his *Welsh Timber Trees* (1930) mentions a pine avenue at Llanvihangel Court in Monmouthshire where the trees were known to be 200 years old and local tradition asserted a historic connection with the Jacobite cause. The original pines were lost, but the present owner has planted a new avenue. Similarly, Lord Dynevor related a similar story to the author regarding a prominent pine clump on his estate near Llandeilo. These are good stories, but sadly no written evidence has yet been discovered to corroborate the belief.

Above: The storm-battered remains of the Charley Trees in the deerpark at Dinefwr Castle.
Top right: Scots pine clump near Tregare, Monmouthshire.

The other purpose for these pines is more practical. Their evergreen nature provided a ready signal in the landscape to travellers and drovers, particularly in winter, before the advent of maps and well-maintained highways, not just as a guide to the correct route but also an indication from landowners that grazing for livestock and hospitality was offered to all.

On a somewhat more ethereal level, the great Herefordian inventor, polymath and businessman Alfred Watkins (1855–1935) believed that these pine clumps meshed in with his vision of ley lines – a sudden perception that came to him while travelling the county in 1921, and which he described as, 'a flood of ancestral memory'. In essence he believed that a network of ancient physical and metaphysical pathways lay within the landscape and were traceable through the straight lines linking features such as churches, standing stones, ancient hill forts and churches, as well as these pines.

Monmouth Catalpa

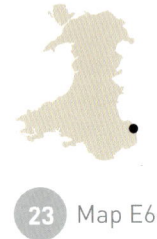

23 Map E6

All over Britain there are many fine landmark trees that have been planted on village greens and in town squares, and have long been held in deep affection by the local communities. An English oak, Britain's iconic broadleaf, was often the choice for such a centrepiece. The spreading horse chestnut with its impressive floral display in spring and conkers for the village children in autumn has been another favourite. Discovering an Indian bean tree (*Catalpa bignonioides*) taking on this role is an altogether singular occurrence and something of a mystery.

The 'Indian' part of the tree's common name is derived from the American Indian association; their name for the tree – *kutuhlpa*, hence Catalpa. The tree is native to the southern states of North America, principally Georgia, Florida, Alabama and Mississippi. While 'bean' might seem to indicate that the fruits are something edible, they are not; it is simply a reference to the shape of the long green seed pods. The naturalist and illustrator Mark Catesby (1682–1749) brought the tree back to Britain and into cultivation here in 1726, after his second tour of the United States. It has since been grown purely for ornamental purposes in parks, gardens and streets and, although quite unrelated, its showy white flowers do bear a passing resemblance to the horse chestnut. Its timber, which is hard and brittle, has few uses.

In St. James' Square, in the middle of Monmouth, a magnificent specimen known locally as 'the Monmouth Catalpa' grows within the iron railing confines that also contain the town's cenotaph – a memorial to all those brave souls lost in the Great War. The tree has become synonymous with the cenotaph, although it was already well established when the monument was unveiled in 1921. The consensus locally is that the tree was planted around 1900, but information is vague, and its size in the 1920s seems to indicate an earlier date. Who would choose such an unusual species of tree for this purpose, and why, and when exactly was it planted? Is there an American connection here?

In 2005 officialdom threatened the tree's existence. In its wisdom Monmouthshire County Council decided that the old tree had to be felled as it posed a threat from branches potentially falling on people and they were worried about the resulting possibility of litigation. At this time there was no history of the tree ever having shed branches, and one suspects it was simply a knee-jerk reaction to the knowledge of similar incidents elsewhere in Britain. The local community was furious and soon Monmouth Town Council,

The Monmouth Catalpa in full flower in July in St. James Square.

Monmouth Action Group and the local Archaeological Society joined forces to oppose the plan to fell. They engaged expert arboriculturist Roy Finch to check the tree and he concluded that with a little remedial attention it would be perfectly safe and should survive for many more years. To quote Roy, it is, 'an outstanding part of our tree heritage and worthy of the effort and expense involved in its management'. A second arboriculturist, Dr. David Lonsdale, also supported the view that the tree was in good shape and in no imminent risk of collapse. The County Council tried to counter these findings, commissioning their own expert to carry out a survey. The conclusion was much the same, except their arboriculturist doubted that the tree would survive the trauma of remedial work, and so recommended felling. Still, the local community felt vindicated in their tussle with the County Council. If the tree did go into serious decline then surely that would be the time to consider felling, not now when it

Left: The exotic flowers
of the Indian bean tree.

was apparently in excellent health. Studying the correspondence and press cuttings of the day, the acrimony and distress amongst the local community is palpable still.

A bizarre incident occurred in the wake of all this upheaval when a local pensioner, Jack Roocroft, infamous in the town for his impulsive actions and an abiding abhorrence of red tape, crept into the square very early one morning, put a ladder against the tree, and chain-sawed off what was considered the offending and potentially dangerous overhanging bough – instant tree surgery which he and many locals believed would finally put pay to the County Council's health and safety argument.

Public pressure finally won the day when the County Council agreed to prop the tree with steel poles – not the most beautiful course of action, but seemingly effective. There are moves afoot at present to try and replace these with oak poles, which would be aesthetically more pleasing. Ultimately, this is a heart-warming story of the people's voice being heard (eventually) and people power overcoming the steamroller of Council officialdom. This Catalpa is probably one of the oldest and largest of its species in Britain and, even though saving such an unusual and special tree has been a battle, it has been well worth the fight.

Caeryder Oak

24 Map D6

Monumental and far-famed oaks have come and gone over the years. Often, the accounts from the nineteenth century show that they were felled for their timber – to satisfy the high demands of the day for oak for shipbuilding and construction. Sadly, other great trees were lost to storms, fires or simply the decrepitude of old age. It seems that the Caeryder Oak falls into the last category.

On the slopes of the Llanhennock ridge, just north of Caerleon and overlooking the lower Usk Valley, the bleached carcass of the once mighty Caeryder Oak stands in a pasture opposite Pencraig Farm. The field is known as Ryder's Field, and so the oak's name derived from *Cae* (Welsh for field) Ryder.

'Early renditions of Wales' most famous trees are difficult to find, but the Caeryder Oak first comes into view in 1834 in a splendid lithograph from a drawing by E.A. Leyson.'

Early renditions of Wales' most famous trees are difficult to find, but the Caeryder Oak first comes into view in 1834 in a splendid lithograph from a drawing by E.A. Leyson. Conveniently, this print also supplies detailed statistics of the tree's dimensions. Its girth at one foot was 38.5 feet (11.7 metres), its height was 70 feet (21.3 metres) and the spread of the boughs extended to 126 feet (38.4 metres). It was already recognised as the largest oak tree in Monmouthshire.

Fame obviously attended this oak, causing it very soon after to come to prominence in a remarkable lithograph from 1838 taken from a painting by H.F. Worsley, which features the coronation fête of Queen Victoria beneath its spreading boughs. Clearly, the assembled crowd are besporting themselves with much jollity; a harpist plays at the foot of the great bole, a bower has been created close by that appears to house a table or perhaps a small informal altar for an impromptu service of thanksgiving for the monarch. We are left to draw our own conclusions. The tree, although partially stag-headed,

Lithograph from 1838 taken from a painting by H.F. Worsley.

seems to be in fine fettle, and the ever present Penycaemawr rises majestically in the distance.

H.A. Hyde, in his *Welsh Timber Trees* (1930), regarded it as, 'probably the largest oak in South Wales.' He recorded its girth at ground level as exceeding 45 feet (13.7 metres) and also revealed that the tree was a hybrid oak (*Quercus petraea x robur*). A photograph of the tree at the time shows a reasonable if slightly thinning canopy.

By 1964, when local historian and writer Fred Hando visited the tree, he was able to measure its girth once more and discovered that it was now some 48 feet (14.6 metres) around. A sketch he made at the time seems to show that there was still some life left in the old tree.

Spread of Branches 156
Estimated Height 90

Caeryder Oak
Glen Uske
Monmouthshire

Circumference at 1 feet from the ground 36½
D.º at the smallest part 21

supposed to be of 600 years
growth.

'Dead it may be, but it is still a link to many centuries of local history and, undoubtedly, an object of sculptural beauty.'

Above: A lithograph of the Caeryder Oak by E.A. Leyson, 1834.

Today, the nearby villagers don't seem to recall any signs of life for at least the last 20 years, but they maintain a deep affection for the old stager. Dead it may be, but it is still a link to many centuries of local history and, undoubtedly, an object of sculptural beauty. It has also become a haven for invertebrate life and even a home for young hollies and rowans sprung from berries dropped in crevices by birds. A strange coincidence occurred in 2010 when the famous Ryder Cup golf tournament was played at the nearby Celtic Manor course.

Curley Oak

25 Map E6

Until quite recently the existence and whereabouts of this ancient oak pollard was known only to a very few people. Sitting forlornly amid the massed ranks of conifers in the middle of Wentwood Forest the Curley Oak was a forgotten and neglected tree.

Wentwood is not a forest that immediately comes to mind for most people. Almost everyone is familiar with the New Forest, Sherwood Forest and even the Forest of Dean, just over the Welsh border in Gloucestershire, but most people would be hard pressed to say where Wentwood Forest might be. Today the remaining 3,000 acres of a wooded area that found first mention during the Dark Ages as Coit Guent (the woods of Gwent), in *The Book of Llandaff*, straddles the hills between the Usk Valley and the Wye Valley, just north of a line between Newport and Chepstow.

For most of the twentieth century Wentwood has been almost completely given over to a giant conifer plantation, subjugating almost all of the original broadleaf woodland. However in 2006, as a result of an ambitious campaign launched by the Woodland Trust, £1.5 million was raised to secure 900 acres of the forest with the avowed intent of returning it to something approaching its original broadleaf structure. During this process some of the last vestiges of the pre-coniferisation forest were uncovered, with the great old Curley Oak being perhaps the oldest surviving inhabitant.

'Sitting forlornly amid the massed ranks of conifers in the middle of Wentwood Forest the Curley Oak was a forgotten and neglected tree.'

Nobody knows for sure how the tree acquired its name. The only suggestion proffered so far is that during the nineteenth century, when map surveyors often asked local inhabitants what the familiar name for a specific feature might be, someone had referred to this tree as the Curley Oak.

Since work has begun to remove many of the conifers the foresters have thinned out some of those which were in very close confines to the oak, letting in more light and reducing the competition for water and nutrients. This is a process that has to be done gradually since the old tree has been surrounded and, to some degree, protected from windblast and full sunlight for the last

few decades. Sudden or dramatic changes to an ancient tree's habitat could cause trauma and result in its demise, so it's very much a case of a little and often with the paring back of the surrounding conifers to maximise its chance of survival. Like most oaks of this size and age it is hollow, and much of the outer shell has perished too, but as long as there is some living tissue to nourish the canopy it must be hoped that this landmark tree will manage to stay with us a good while yet.

Chepstow Aspen

26 Map E6

If you were told that the biggest tree in Britain covered more than an acre, and yet it didn't have a massive trunk 30 or 40 feet in girth, you might be puzzled. If you were also told that this tree wasn't an oak or a beech or a yew or, for that matter, even a Douglas fir or a giant redwood, you might wonder where to start. If you were finally told that this species of tree has been known to live 10,000 years and that one tree, growing from a single original rootstock, in the Wasatch Mountains of Utah, covers about 106 acres you would be totally confused.

Aspen is perhaps a more famous and prolific native species in North America – the city of Aspen, Colorado taking its name from the locally abundant American aspen (*Populus tremuloides*). Britain's native aspen (*Populus tremula*), which also occurs across a huge range throughout Europe, is not one of the country's most prominent species, usually confined to hedges or woods and seldom seen as large stands or open-grown individual trees. It's only when you get into the highlands of Scotland that you begin to notice its presence in any great order. So it seems rather unusual to happen upon this landmark tree tucked away by the side of one of the fairways on a golf course near Chepstow, in Monmouthshire.

The golf course is part of St. Pierre Hotel and Country Club, which was a country estate until the 1960s, attached to a grand house with fourteenth century origins. All around the old parkland, which has now become two golf courses, stand impressive specimen trees. There are public footpaths here and, as long as you keep your wits about you for flying golf balls, it's a wonderful place to enjoy some splendid trees. The walk across the fairways to find the aspen takes in some massive sweet chestnuts, which must be well over 300 years old. When you find the aspen you might be forgiven for being rather underwhelmed. It looks rather like a small woodland of densely grouped stems. The natural regeneration that produces this appearance is suckering, for since aspen seldom sets much viable seed in Britain the tree has taken to reproducing by throwing up a multitude of suckers. This 'woodland' of well over an acre and comprising of several thousand stems originates from one single tree, which might well have grown here in excess of 1,000 years ago. To prove this, a DNA fingerprint can be taken from a variety of these stems and they will all be found to match. Obviously the original tree's bole is long gone, but its progeny march on forever.

Pontypool
Sweet Chestnuts

27 Map D6

East of the town centre of Pontypool there lies 150 acres of beautiful landscaped park, known affectionately to the locals as the People's Park. However, it hasn't always been the wonderful public amenity that it is today; for these were private pleasure grounds of a wealthy and powerful industrialist of the eighteenth century.

Major John Hanbury, a local ironmaster, inherited Park House and its estate from his father in 1701, soon afterwards beginning an extensive remodelling of the surrounding parkland; an area that today encompasses Pontypool or People's Park. In the small valley in the middle of the park there was originally one large pond, fed from streams on the hills above, which would have functioned as a head of water to drop further down into the valley to power the Hanbury forges. Early maps, made shortly after the landscaping of the park, show avenues of sweet chestnut and beech following the contours of the valley up towards the folly tower.

In 1920 the local authority was able to purchase the grounds of Park House, and the last Squire of Pontypool, John Capel Hanbury, formally transferred ownership at a Great Fête on the Easter Monday, when 15,000 people turned out to hear Mr. Hanbury proclaim it henceforth to be People's Park.

Today, the single pond has become the two separate ponds of Nant-y-Gollen Ponds. There is little sign of any ancient beech trees, but then over 300 years would be rather exceptional for their survival, particularly if they were maiden trees. However, there are a few ancient sweet chestnut pollards along either side of the ponds, some a little more decrepit than others, but still hanging in there none the less. Park rangers estimate that these trees could be about 400 years old, which would mean that they predate the Hanbury landscaping. From their size, when compared to other chestnuts elsewhere known to be 400 years old, one might put these nearer 350 years, which would take them back to the mid-seventeenth century when the estate was established. Tradition asserts that these trees were pollarded to provide charcoal for the iron forges along the Afon Lwyd. This was probably a convenient use for the loppings, but they wouldn't have kept the forges going for very long in their own right; huge quantities of coppice wood were required for this purpose.

Some of the chestnuts have hollowed, their cadaverous old forms clinging to life by a thread, while others look extremely hale, throwing out vibrant new growth after they have been trimmed back, so they should go on for a long time yet. It is hard to think of any other municipal parks across Wales that can boast such a splendid group of ancient trees.

Mamhilad Yew

(28) Map D6

Above: Engraving of The Mamhilad Yew from *Arboretum et Fruticetum Britannicum* 1838.

In the little village of Mamhilad, and just to the north of Pontypool, a stone's throw from the bustling A4042, stands the modest church of St. Illtyd, marooned in a dark green tide of yew trees. One of these, a female tree standing opposite the south porch, is one of Wales' mightiest yews.

In 1799 Archdeacon Coxe recorded a visit in his *Historical Tour of Monmouth*, when he found '12 fine yews.' A little later, in 1838, John Claudius Loudon considered this yew worthy of more detailed observation in his *Arboretum et Fruticetum Britannicum*:

'The Mamhilad Yew stands in the churchyard of Mamhilad, a few miles north of Pontypool: it is a female; and, 2 feet 6 inches from the ground, where the trunk has a fair medium thickness, it measures 29 feet 4 inches in circumference. At about 4 feet high, it divides into six main boughs, one of which is quite decayed. The trunk is hollow; and, on the north side, it has an opening down to the ground, which is gradually contracting on both sides by annual deposits of new wood. Within this opening, and in the centre of the original tree, is seen another, and apparently detached, yew, several feet in diameter, covered with bark, and in a state of vigorous growth: it is, in fact, of itself a great tree, and overtops the old one. On examination, however, it is found to be united behind, and also at some distance from the ground, by two great contorted arms, one on each side, to the inner wall of its decaying parent; being a curious example of natural inarching, and having altogether a very striking and singular appearance.'

'The great old Mamhilad Yew squats atop a shallow mound, banked up with boulders all around...'

Loudon's account clearly mentions the internal stem or tree within a tree, which he describes, with its connecting arms, as inarching. He appears to have thought that, as the new tree grew within, it then fused with the inside of the old tree. What he perhaps overlooked was that this form was more than likely caused by aerial roots which had grown down from inside the old bole, made contact with the earth, taken root, and then grown up again as the new inner stem; in essence the process in reverse. Strictly speaking inarching is the coalescence of two boughs from separate plants or trees forming a union of tissue; a sort of mutual graft. This can happen naturally and is often observed in beech trees.

Loudon does furnish his reader with a delightful little engraving of the tree, where the central stem is most clearly delineated, and bears comparison with the form of the tree evident today. In 1895 the Rev. Christopher Cook remarked upon the 'twelve yew-trees in the churchyard', but today only five remain, although thankfully the largest tree is one of those survivors.

The great old Mamhilad Yew squats atop a shallow mound, banked up with boulders all around, and although it is still in fine fettle, its six main boughs in Loudon's day have now become just four. Measurements taken recently make it 31 feet 3 inches (9.53 m.) at the base, so perhaps a little larger than 1838. Popular opinion seems to endow this yew with an age of about 2,500 years.

Bute Park

29 Map D6

Above: Flowering
cherry tree.
Right: Wonderful
convoluted and
buttressed bole of
a dawn redwood.

Remarkable individual trees are the main thrust of this book, but it would be churlish to overlook the many impressive collections and arboreta in Wales. Many of these are still private gardens and must surely possess a host of little known and noteworthy specimens. However, there are plenty of private gardens which open to the public on an occasional basis, the splendid gardens and parks of Wales' great houses in the custodianship of the National Trust or Cadw, and of course the numerous municipal parks which are freely available to one and all throughout the year. Bute Park, in the centre of Cardiff, is arguably one of the finest public parks in the whole of Britain, and famed for its wonderful collection of trees.

The park was originally laid out between 1873 and 1901 by Andrew Pettigrew, head gardener to the third Marquess of Bute, as the pleasure ground for the nearby castle and home of the Marquess. Pettigrew was a Scotsman, and it is remarkable to see how many Scots worked for the largest Welsh estates throughout the nineteenth century. Of course, the Bute estates extended to Scotland, which is an obvious explanation for this connection, but Dr. Linnard remarks upon a generation of skilled foresters in Scotland from the late eighteenth century onwards in his *Welsh Woods and Forests*:

1. One of the splendid London planes at the southern end of Bute Park.
2. A Japanese hop hornbeam, noted for its wide spreading form.
3. Autumn tints beneath a stand of birches.
4. The startling early spring foliage of sunrise horse chestnut.
5. Japanese maple
6. Remarkable variety of mosses and lichens on one of the maples.

One of the impressive old London planes
in Bute Park, touched with autumnal gold.

'The pre-eminence of Scots foresters in experience and reputation is reflected in the way in which they were sought after for positions in Wales and elsewhere – it was both fashionable and practical to employ Scots as foresters on Welsh estates.'

In 1947 the fifth Marquess presented the park, castle and nearby Sophia Gardens (just across the River Taff) to Cardiff Council, which still owns and manages the park today. In the same year William Nelmes, then director of the Parks Department, began the planting of the arboretum. Extending to 130 acres (56 hectares), Bute Park is a glorious green lung for the busy city, with more than 2,000 trees, over 40 of which are national champions, including many rare species.

It provides a wonderful selection of urban habitats for wildlife, with frequent sightings of woodpeckers, kingfishers, tree creepers and, near the river, otters, herons and egrets. The park is also home to a great many grey squirrels. Cute they may be, but they can take their toll on the trees. The purity of the air, even in the midst of a big city, is reflected in the luxuriant growth of mosses and lichens, their varied forms and colours clothing many of the tree trunks.

Various tree collections in the park come into their own at different times of year. The flowering cherries are superb in early spring, while the Japanese maples are the crowning glory of autumn with their rich array of fiery colours. Perhaps the most impressive of the larger trees are the massive London planes at the southern end of the park – their towering canopies glorious in verdant, spring green or autumnal gold; the distinctive plated, mottled bark on their resolute boles. Their impressive size surely indicates that they pre-date the Victorian ornamental landscaping, as they could easily be 200 years old. At the northern reaches of the park it is certainly worth seeking out the glorious ruddy, buttressed boles of the dawn redwoods – a fossil tree only rediscovered in China in 1941. After its introduction to Britain in 1949 it was much planted and it seems to thrive here.

There's always something going on in the park. As well as the various wood sculptures dotted around there are exhibitions, concerts, sporting events and a lively educational programme contributing to the busy calendar. There is a cracking restaurant at the Summerhouse Kiosk and simply bags of space to wind down and chill out in the midst of the big city, all of which goes to make Bute Park so much more than the sum of its parts.

True Service Tree

30 Map D7

On the limestone cliffs of south Wales, near the port and resort of Barry, three very small wild colonies of an exceptionally rare tree of the *Sorbus* tribe may be found. The true service tree (*Sorbus domestica*) is easily confused with either the rowan (*Sorbus aucuparia*) or the ash (*Fraxinus excelsior*), because of the great similarity of the leaves, but its distinctive fruits, like little clusters of small ruddy pears, clinch its identity.

The tree is a native species of southern and central Europe and the western fringes of Asia, but has long been the subject of debate concerning its native status in Britain.

It is thought that the earliest reference to what must surely be the true service tree dates back to the writings of a Welsh monk called Nennius, who compiled a short list of Marvels of Britain (De Mirabilibus Britanniae) in his *Historia Brittonum* of 829. The translation from the Latin in essence reads: 'by the river which is called Guoy [Wye] apples are found on an ash tree on the declivity of the wood which is near the mouth of the river'. There are two slightly different forms of the species – pyrifera resembles small pears and pomifera resembles small apples, this latter perhaps bearing out this early reference.

'...the earliest reference to what must surely be the true service tree dates back to the writings of a Welsh monk called Nennius...'

Probably due to its very restricted distribution in Britain little is written of the tree by most eighteenth-and nineteenth-century authorities. The only significant example to attract attention was the Whitty Pear (an alternative name) discovered in the middle of the Wyre Forest by one Alderman Edmund Pitts of Worcester in 1678. In his account of what he described as S*orbus pyriformis* he remarks on the fruit as being, '... in September so rough as to be ready to strangle one. But being then gathered, and kept till October they eat as well as any medlar.' This description vindicates another of the tree's alternative epithets of Choke Pear. When the fruits have been allowed to blet (over-ripen or rot) they become sweeter and softer, and have often been used to make a cider-like drink. It has been asserted that this use has prompted the name 'service' – from *cerevisia*; while Grigson proffers an alternative derivation from *sevres*, plural of *sevre*, from OE *syrfe*, from the Latin *Sorbus*. The famous Whitty Pear succumbed to a vandal who burnt it down in 1862, but many planted specimens still grow in Worcestershire, although only one, at Arley Castle, is thought to have been derived from a cutting struck from the old tree.

The redoubtable Loudon has much to say of the tree in his *Arboretum et Fruticetum Britannicum* of 1844. There is ample reference to the Wyre Forest tree, and reference to a large tree in the garden of John Tradescant at Lambeth, but no mention of the tree growing wild in Wales. The timber was clearly prized for all manner of demanding tasks in France – particularly, 'by millwrights, for making cogs to wheels, rollers, cylinders, blocks and pulleys, spindles and axles; and for those parts of machines which are subject to much friction, and require great strength and durability ... also for the screws to wine-presses ...

'...they grow on sheer and unstable cliffs, often amid much dense undergrowth.'

In Britain, the wood is almost unknown; though if it were to be imported, it might probably be used as a substitute for box [for turnery and engravers' blocks].'

So, native or not? Study of the Welsh trees has ascertained that the oldest examples are around 400 years old – remarkable, considering their relatively modest size. There are theories that the tree was cultivated in early monastic gardens, or perhaps that it might even have been introduced by the Romans. Since its first discovery at Porthkerry Country Park in 1983 opinions on its native status have wavered. In the intervening years more trees have been located further along the Glamorgan coastline and several others over in Gloucestershire, around the Severn estuary. Current thinking is that these trees should all be regarded as 'persistant escapees from cultivation.' However, this is by no means the last word on the matter and, particularly if further wild communities of the trees are discovered, there may still be scope for reconsideration.

It cannot be stated too strongly, that if you go looking for these trees then extreme caution should be exercised as they grow on sheer and unstable cliffs, often amid much dense undergrowth. The location at Aberthaw, where the trees can be viewed on the cliffs from the shingle beach, is perhaps the safest place to recommend.

Above: Cliff face above
the beach at Aberthaw.

Silent Valley Beeches

31 Map D6

The setting may not immediately appear to be the most promising place to find an exciting wood where special trees flourish, but the Silent Valley, wedged as it is between the grey terraces of Cwm, just south of Ebbw Vale, and the rumble and stench of a massive refuse landfill site, is still well worth a look.

The woods of Cwm Merddog and beyond, at the head of the valley, Coed Tyn-y-gelli (SSSI status) are recognised as the most westerly and highest altitude native beech woodlands in Britain. Here you may find craggy old beech pollards with massive, convoluted roots and long-neglected coppice stools hanging precariously from deeply cut banks. These are not pure beech woods, for oak, birch and, in the wetter flushes, alder may be found. The beeches are the stars here – huge deliriously contorted specimens, shaped by many cycles of wood-cutting, the elements and great age, for some of these trees may easily be as much as 300 years old.

'...massive, convoluted roots and long-neglected coppice stools hanging precariously from deeply cut banks.'

With the onset of the Industrial Revolution more than 200 years ago, a once-tranquil farming landscape was catapulted into a mining bonanza; the Silent Valley must have been anything but silent. There are remnants of the old tramline (or dramline, as it was known locally) still evident along the hillside above the wood, where coal from the opencast or drift mines was transported down the valley. Plentiful evidence of coppicing and pollarding, more so the latter, indicates that sheep were frequently grazed up here. Wood was cut for fuel as well as for charcoal to charge the forges of the ironworks, but little or no beech appears to have been cut for many a year.

Although this policy of low-level intervention currently maintains the remarkable characteristics of the beeches there will come a point where a succession of decay and decline will mean that these trees will eventually be lost. It is the regular harvesting hand of man that has preserved them so that we can be intrigued by their forms today, and it would seem that some more judicious management will be the only way to take them further into the future.

Ley's Whitebeam

32 Map D6

Rev. Augustin Ley
(1842 –1911)

One of the rarest trees in Britain, indeed one of the rarest trees in the world, is Ley's whitebeam (*Sorbus leyana*). It may not have the stature of a veteran oak or the mystique of an ancient yew, but these little trees, of which only 13 specimens are known in the wild, are equally remarkable.

When not attending to his clerical duties The Reverend Augustin Ley (1842–1911) reserved most of his time for pursuing his avid interest in botanical studies. His father, also a clergyman, imbued the young Augustin with a passion for botany which would become an abiding obsession. Records show that he travelled extensively around his Herefordshire home, where he was curate at Sellack and Kings Caple, also doing much botanising in south Wales, Shropshire and Yorkshire. Ley was also one of the editors for the 1889 *A Flora of Herefordshire*. As well as his studies of trees and flowers he seems to be particularly celebrated for his in-depth bryological (study of mosses and liverworts) surveys and discoveries.

Ley was systematically searching the whole area for hawkweeds (*Hieracium* sp.), when he came across the rare whitebeams, which we now know as Ley's whitebeam, in the upper Taff Valley in 1896. He had already explored other limestone crags in the southern Brecon Beacons in earlier years, in 1893 realising that the lesser whitebeam (*Sorbus minima*) was something out of the ordinary. One can only assume that his natural curiosity led him in search of other variations on the whitebeam theme. Ley discovered the tree on the cliffs of Darren Fach, on the east side of the valley. He thought it was *Pyrus scandica*, Swedish whitebeam (now known as *Sorbus intermedia*) and it was known by this name until reclassified by the botanist A.J. Wilmott in 1934 as *Sorbus leyana*, in honour of the man who first discovered it. It derives from a natural crossing of rowan (*Sorbus aucuparia*) with rock whitebeam (*Sorbus rupicola*) or perhaps grey-leaved whitebeam (*Sorbus porrigentiformis*).

The two locations where the tree is found today are extremely precipitous and dangerous, where the small trees grow out of crevices in the limestone, safe from the attentions of sheep, deer and rabbits. Ley must have risked life and limb to get close enough to examine these plants in detail and to obtain herbarium specimens. Either that, or in his day perhaps there were more trees; however it can't have been many more for Ley only reported seeing '15–20 mostly inaccessible shrubs'. It was to be more than half a century before J.O. Evans discovered three more of these trees hidden away on

Above: The leaf shape shows the influence of the rock whitebeam and rowan from which Ley's whitebeam is derived.
Left: Ley's whitebeam, perched on the edge of limestone crags above the Taff Valley.

Penmoelallt, on the western side of the valley. In 1963 the Forestry Commission decided to try and help the species along by planting seven saplings grown from Penmoelallt seeds on the top of cliffs above the original colony. Six survive to this day, and are faring well as 30 foot trees.

In the interest of their conservation, we will not pinpoint their exact location. There is always the risk that excessive visitor pressure may compromise their habitat. There is also evidence that, in 1996, someone visited the site and dug up a sapling: since Ley's whitebeam is currently classified internationally as 'Critically Endangered', if caught, they would be subject to the full force of the law.

Llangorse Wych Elm

33 Map D5

Elms, in general, have become a rare sight in the landscape since the onset of the dreaded Dutch elm disease in the early 1970s which continues to ravage the British elm population. Large English elms (*Ulmus minor* var. *vulgaris*) and smooth-leaved, narrow-leaved, small-leaved or field elm (*Ulmus minor*) were two omnipresent species until disease decimated them; their main downfall being that they are clonal species, usually reproducing from suckers, so that large populations often grow from common root systems or, even when growing individually, they are of exactly the same genetic form as their neighbours. This means that when disease strikes there has been no genetic diversity to offer the hope of selective resistance, so whole colonies of trees die. However, wych elm (*Ulmus glabra*) has had rather better fortune than most of its cousins.

The wych elm is commonly regarded as the only native elm species in Britain. It does not reproduce by suckering, and trees do have a genetic diversity, which has helped it to resist Dutch elm disease. Also the fact that there are small colonies and individual trees in many quite isolated locations has kept them out of reach of the beetles that carry the disease. Like the other elms, wych elm flowers in early spring, producing its vivid green fruits which look from a distance like a flush of new leaves. As the fruits ripen the actual foliage soon follows on, and in this species the leaves are quite distinctive, often being as much as six inches long, shorter stemmed than other elms, with a central leading tip and shouldered cusps or horns on either side.

'...the largest elm in Wales'

Above: The burry base of the Llangorse wych elm bristles with epicormic shoots.

Wych elm normally grows in woodland, frequently found as coppice stools, and occasionally occurs as a hedgerow tree. Single open-grown specimens of wych elm are relatively rare, so to find this old pollard growing on the edge of pasture above the village of Llangorse was something of an unusual discovery. Clearly the tree has long been cut as a pollard because browsing livestock find elm foliage particularly palatable and would soon strip the tree if they could reach the new growth. This tree has an impressive girth of 14 feet (4.3 metres), making it, according to The Tree Register, the largest elm in Wales. Activity by the Ancient Tree Hunt in recent years to locate Britain's oldest and largest trees has only managed to register 16 notable elms from across the whole of Wales on its database, suggesting that they have become something of a rarity.

Llanfeugan Yew Circle

34 Map D5

The tiny settlement of Llanfeugan isn't marked on Ordnance Survey maps, but it lies about half a mile to the west of the village of Pencelli, south-east of Brecon, where the dramatic slopes of the Brecon Beacons sweep far above to the immediate south. In the remote churchyard of St. Meugan, wandering amongst the ancient yews which almost completely enfold the little church, it is easy to lose track of the rest of the world; entranced by the writhing, sculptural forms of each highly individual bole, lulled by birdsong and the gentle swish of the breeze through the dark fronds above.

The first mention of the yews here comes in Lewis's *Topographical Dictionary of Wales* for 1834, but then they seem to have faded back into obscurity, for neither John Lowe in his 1897 work on yews, nor Vaughan Cornish in 1946, remark upon them.

'...entranced by the writing, sculptural forms of each highly individual bole...'

Above / below:
Two different views
of the largest yew in
the circle.

The 12 yews that encircle the church are of varying size, but this form alone would seem to signify a pre-Christian site. Certainly the oldest tree, to the north-east of the church, with an impressive girth of 29 feet 8 inches (9.0 metres) at ground level will predate the foundation of the first church here in the seventh century. This male tree is an absolute gem, divided into three massive trunks. Recent measurements have even pushed its girth in excess of 30 feet (9.1 metres), but then there will always be minor anomalies with gaining exact statistics of such eccentric forms.

This remote location may be a little off the beaten track, but the tranquil, magical nature of the place makes it well worth seeking out.

Brecon Black Poplar

The native black poplar (*Populus nigra* subsp. *betulifolia*) has achieved a particularly high profile amongst native broadleaf trees in recent years. Largely due to the work of Edgar Milne-Redhead in the 1970s and 80s, the plight of native black poplars was brought to the forefront of public awareness. Back then it seemed as if this tree had been slowly disappearing from the nation's all too-short inventory of native broadleaf species, for most of them were getting old (few having been planted in the last 150 years), and the chance of naturally occurring new trees was slender due to a massive sex imbalance. The male trees vastly outnumbered the females and frequently both sexes existed in isolation, making the chances of pollination a tenuous affair. The other problem was that due to vast quantities of introduced poplar clones the genetic purity of the species was virtually impossible to guarantee – all poplars being highly prone to hybridising.

'...the largest black poplar in Britain...'

The Daily Telegraph's 'Black Poplar Hunt' of 1994 reinvigorated the drive to identify exactly how many trees there might be in the country. Early indications looked bleak, with barely a couple of thousand trees identified. Eighteen years on, and with the benefit of many eagle-eyed 'poplar hunters' current best estimates are around 7,000 trees, although this is still not very many when considered in a national context. Old trees are often lost as they decline and die, but thankfully many of the oldest trees are pollards and by regularly reinstigating this management regime they should carry on a lot longer. Even though widespread land drainage for agriculture has not helped these floodplain trees, recent emphasis on caring for hedgerow trees, and a general move towards hedge conservation should help; for this is the usual habitat for the trees. The sexual imbalance of the species is just as bad as it was 40 years ago, so a carefully controlled programme is now in place to produce genuine, genetically authentic trees. Females will be planted in the company of males, and there are even plans to recreate the damp floodplain conditions which would favour black poplar woodland – a landscape feature long since lost from the British countryside.

'...a unique geometry which makes it stand out from its hybrid cousins...'

The black poplar depicted here stands on the edge of school playing fields in Brecon, Powys. It displays the archetypal profile of the tree, with arched boughs and leaning bole; a unique geometry which makes it stand out from its hybrid cousins, and readily identifiable throughout the leafless months. A male tree, this particular specimen is the largest black poplar in Britain, with a girth of 21 feet 6 inches (6.5 metres), and standing a mighty 110 feet high.

While photographing the tree a couple of teachers from the school walked past and told me that the whole school and many people in the local community were greatly aware of the exceptional nature of this special tree. It is the last surviving member of a row of black poplars. In recent years cuttings have been taken and planted nearby, so that if storms ever lay it low then genetically authentic descendants will take the line forward.

Rhandirmwyn Oak

36 Map C5

The upper Tywi Valley still has a great sense of remoteness. Small, intimate communities and farms snuggled among the hills, linked by narrow lanes, little changed for perhaps the last 400 years; familiar and vital to the locals; ripe with intrigue and adventure for the visitors. For a while, in the eighteenth and nineteenth centuries, there was a vibrant lead mining industry up here, at its peak employing more than 400 men, but this all petered out in the early twentieth century. There are many fine broadleaf trees in the valley, but much of the uplands have been transmuted with great swathes of conifers.

'It is such a splendid old stager and much bigger than any other oak for some distance around, that everyone can point you in the right direction.'

Above: Brigyn play their song 'Popeth yn ei le' inside the hollow Rhandirmwyn Oak in 2005.

Seeking the famous Rhandirmwyn Oak in the village doesn't take very long. It is such a splendid old stager and much bigger than any other oak for some distance around that everyone can point you in the right direction. It sits on the side of the lane that leads across the valley from the village centre, above Pwllpriddog Farm, on the road towards Cilycwm. Even though it has been there for 600–700 years nobody can actually tell you why it is celebrated other than for its size, a very respectable 27 feet 6 inches (8.4 metres). Enquiries at the local pub – the Royal Oak, no less – still draw a blank.

Like many other aged oaks this tree is a pollard, clearly neglected of late it is to be wondered whether a gentle trimming back might not help it into later life. Ivy has done its work in the past and, even though someone thought to relieve the old oak of its load, the dead trailing stems of the plant still ensnare the boughs; but ivy is relentless and it is on its way up the old bole again with renewed vigour. The oak is also playing host to a couple of quite handsome little aerial holly trees, sprung from the droppings (of one sort or another) of some visiting birds. It is always amazing to think that these little colonizers can find enough nutrients to survive.

After my visit a chance communication from Rory Francis from the Woodland Trust recommended a viewing of the website of Welsh language singing duo Brigyn, whose name, incidentally, means 'branch' – reflecting the band's 'primary connection to trees and nature'. It transpired that the brothers Ynyr and Eurig Roberts, who hail from Snowdonia, were shown the oak by their friend Liz Fleming-Williams and, awestruck, they instantly thought it would be an amazing experience to perform a song inside the old tree. Having sought permission from the owner, they managed to wriggle inside and play their song 'Popeth yn ei le' (Everything in its place); filming it as part of the promotional launch for their 2005 album "Brigyn 2". So now the tree has acquired a very modern and perhaps unique strand of fame.

To check out the wonderful sounds of Brigyn go to www.brigyn.com

Defynnog Yew

37 Map D5

A few miles to the west of Brecon and a little to the south of Sennybridge lies the village of Defynnog. Four splendid ancient yews may be found in the large churchyard of the fifteenth-century St. Cynog's church which lies on the slope between the village and the gurgling waters of the River Senni below. These are all female trees although, strangely, a few years back Tim Hills of the Ancient Yew Group discovered a male bough on the largest of the four. This is not an unknown phenomenon, but it is fairly uncommon.

The largest tree of these four craggy survivors is usually known as the Defynnog Yew and has recently been measured with a girth of 38 feet (11.6 metres) at 2 feet above ground, but a difficult area of definition between the bole and the widely-splayed, low-set boughs makes claims for this being the largest yew in Wales debatable. Even so, such a size puts the tree firmly in the band of 2,000 – 3,000 years old, making it certainly one of the largest and potentially one of the oldest yews in Wales. Yet it seems rather strange that there are no historical accounts of the tree. In fact it wasn't until the Brecon

Yew Survey of 1970 that the significance of the tree seems to have come to light. With their extreme antiquity it could be surmised that this tree, along with its nearby sisters, which display girths of 28, 25 and 22 feet (8.5, 7.6 and 6.7 metres), might be the remnants of a pre-Christian site. However, even though they stand in an arc formation there is no evidence of a circle of trees or any ancient earthworks to vindicate this suspicion.

Close observation here reveals some odd occurrences. The smallest of the other three trees would appear to have grown as the result of a layered branch from the the Defynnog Yew – a DNA crossmatch would confirm this. Also a tiny sprig of golden foliage is evident on the bole of the great tree (see top right hand corner in the picture opposite). It is possible that this is what is known as a sport; in essence a chance mutation, but the sort of manifestation that has often led to the breeding of such variants as ornamental cultivars. Striking this sprig as a cutting or graft to create an independent plant would test the theory. If it retained its pale colour then it would be a viable genetic variation – almost certainly only reproduceable from further cuttings. However if it reverted to the normal dark green then it must be some physiological effect associated with the parent tree. The explanation for its occurrence remains something of a mystery, although I have also observed it on the Much Marcle Yew in Herefordshire.

Talley Abbey Ash

38 Map C5

Although the ruins of Talley Abbey, set in the peaceful Cothi Valley, are well signposted, there are relatively few visitors to this rural outpost. The abbey, thought to have been founded around 1185, was once a monastery of the Premonstratensian order (the white canons), and has lain in ruins since the dissolution by Henry VIII. It is said that much of the stone was robbed to build the surrounding cottages and farms.

Most visitors will saunter through this romantic ruin, a monument safely in the hands of Cadw, with little inkling that there is a superb green monument only 300 yards away to the east, along a public footpath. A stupendous ash tree

'Trying to gauge the age of such a large ash is extremely difficult...'

(*Fraxinus excelsior*) towering above an old hedgerow has grown to a remarkable size for a species not usually noted for its great longevity. Access for making accurate measurements of this tree's girth is difficult, what with closely confined (and very prickly) hawthorns, a wire fence and a dense sheath of ivy. Working carefully around the many knobbles and undulations the girth at about 5 feet seems to be 24–25 feet (7.3–7.6 metres), making it probably the largest maiden ash tree in Wales. It is actually a twin-stemmed tree, which could mean that the lower part, where measurements are taken, could be two stems fused together, technically limiting its claim to be the largest single-stemmed ash. Yet it surely seems a little pedantic to rob this great tree of its champion mantle.

Trying to gauge the age of such a large ash is extremely difficult, as there are relatively few similar sized ash trees with which to make comparisons. However, an estimate of 200–250 years may not be far off the mark. Other ash trees in Wales, both old pollards in hedgerows as well as ancient coppice stools in woodlands, may not be so visually striking as huge trees, but could easily be even older. Ash responds extremely well to being regularly cut back, and these processes greatly extend the lifespan of broadleaf trees, but as a maiden tree the Talley Abbey Ash is a remarkable survivor.

Dinefwr Oaks

39 Map C5

Hard by the small market town of Llandeilo in Carmarthenshire lies the estate of Dinefwr, with its medieval castle perched high on the hills above the Tywi Valley, handsome seventeenth-century mansion with Victorian gothic remodelling, and surrounding deer park. After something of a chequered history, particularly over the last 50 years when the mansion was almost lost because of its semi-derelict condition, the National Trust acquired the property between 1987 and 1990, and now manage the 707 acre estate, restoring the ailing Newton House, and making both parkland and house into a wonderful attraction as well as a superb centre for cultural events and local functions.

'...the great landscaper Capability Brown was commissioned to work his magic on what must have already been a striking landscape.'

Above: Early morning view down the Tywi Valley from Dinefwr Park.

The deer park would undoubtedly have existed in some form as far back as the medieval period to service the needs of the Lords Rhys but the present landscape was only formally emparked somewhere between 1590 and 1650. Deer parks have never been plentiful in Wales, most of them being closer to the English borderlands, so not only Dinefwr's survival but the mere fact that it was established in the first place makes it very special. After the completion of the park wall in 1774 the great landscaper Capability Brown was commissioned to work his magic on what must have already been a striking landscape. Fashion has often been a fickle master, with former glories so readily disdained, but fortunately a lot of the pre-landscaping trees seem to have survived. Down near the house a handful of ancient sweet chestnuts were obviously picturesque enough by 1775 to be retained.

Above: Derwen Grop –
a bizarre old oak on
Dinefwr Park. Close
inspection of this
Edwardian postcard
indicates that the printers
have ever so slightly
enhanced the image with
the provision of an eye
and a mouth.

Out in the park, large areas of woodland and selective clumps of great old oaks are found in goodly numbers; some of the more obvious clumps presumably a legacy of the Brown landscaping. The low-lying areas are generally given over to grassland for the resident herd of fallow deer. White park cattle, which roamed at Dinefwr for many centuries but were removed when the estate was sold in 1974, have also recently been reintroduced. The very oldest oaks are long neglected pollards, so clearly a wood pasture regime must have been in place prior to the mid-eighteenth century. Most of the oaks under about 200 years of age are maidens, so there would have been some degree of compartmental management latterly to give these trees a fair chance of survival from the deer; indeed some areas are still fenced round

today. Mosses and lichens bedeck many of the trees and the whole park is a rich repository of invertebrates. The views down the Tywi Valley from the western edge of the park are truly magnificent.

On the top most point of the park, to the north-west, stands one of the clumps of Scots pines affectionately known across Wales as Charley Trees (see p.92). In 1935 Lord Dynevor asserted that they had indeed been planted to commemorate the Jacobite rebellion of 1745, but certainly they would have been too small to act as any kind of beacon to a safe haven for sympathizers in the immediate aftermath. Today they are an atmospheric yet storm-battered historic feature of the park.

Golden Grove

40 Map C5

There has been a house of note at Golden Grove since 1570 when the Vaughan family completed their first mansion on raised ground overlooking the Tywi Valley, a little to the west of Llandeilo. In 1804 the last of the Vaughans died without an heir and so the *Gelli Aur* (Golden Grove's Welsh name) estate passed into the hands of the Cawdor family. Between 1827 and 1832 they built the house that still stands to this day. Sadly, the great pile looks a little forlorn now, its grandeur certainly somewhat faded, and not open to the public.

'Believed to have been planted in 1863, barely ten years after the species had arrived from America...'

By contrast, the nearby ten acre arboretum, created by the Cawdor's head gardener William Hill during the 1860s, is still very much open and extremely well managed by an expert gardening team from Carmarthenshire County Council. Noted for its fine displays of rhododendrons and azaleas in May, it also boasts some magnificent specimen trees – particularly some spectacular conifers. There are giant redwoods, Monterey pine, Sitka spruce, Douglas fir and, perhaps most dramatic of all, a massive multi-stemmed western red cedar.

Entering the arboretum and suddenly coming upon this western red cedar (*Thuja plicata*) standing in almost constant deep shade, with only a little dappled sunlight sneaking through the surrounding vegetation, is like discovering some giant's candelabra abandoned in the gloom. Believed to have been planted in 1863, barely 10 years after the species had arrived from America, this formation is not uncommon and was created by pegging down low branches of the young tree with the specific aim of making convenient seating for the family and friends promenading through the arboretum...and it worked very well.

A huge multi-stemmed Douglas fir (*Pseudotsuga menziesii*), a stone's throw from the cedar, appears to have been manipulated in the same manner during its early years, but has not responded in anything like as convenient a manner, and would be anything but comfortable seating. Some have suggested that this may be a bundle-planted tree, but that is unlikely.

There are lots of other beautiful trees to enjoy in the country park – some whiskery old common limes along the driveway, believed to be over one 150 years old, as well as some handsome oaks, sweet chestnuts, and a record girth fern-leaved beech. In the walled garden of the house, unfortunately not accessible, stands one of the largest tulip trees in Britain. However, it is the giant conifers that make Golden Grove so special, since so many of these trees throughout Wales have been lost when the grand houses fell into decline and the families that treasured their gardens and trees could no longer afford the upkeep of their vast estates.

Aberglasney Yew Tunnel

41 Map C5

The house and gardens of Aberglasney, set snugly in the hills to the north of the Tywi Valley, west of Llandeilo, have a richly chequered history dating back to medieval times. Without wishing to set down a complete account here, the reader would be well advised to visit the Aberglasney website to enjoy a splendidly detailed and meticulously researched history of the property.

The one feature of the gardens that has drawn many tree lovers to Aberglasney is the remarkable yew tunnel – a feature thought to be unique in Britain. A row of about six yews were planted roughly 280 years ago by Robert Dyer, son of a Carmarthen lawyer who had bought the estate in 1710, and brother of the celebrated poet John Dyer. Upon their arrival the Dyers instigated a comprehensive programme of rebuilding work to the house which included the Queen Anne-style façade seen today. They also wished to make their mark on the gardens and the planting of the yews was but one element of their influence.

Time passed, and the fortunes of Aberglasney waxed and waned with a variety of owners and their respective financial vicissitudes. After the Second World

'...the remarkable yew tunnel – a feature thought to be unique in Britain.'

War the whole place was slowly sucked into a spiral of decline so that, by 1995, with the house in a parlous state of dereliction and the gardens submerged beneath a tangle of weeds, something dramatic was required to rescue Aberglasney before it was lost forever.

A group of local people who had monitored the late decline of the property came together in 1995 to form the Aberglasney Restoration Trust and, with the help of money kindly donated by an American benefactor, were able to purchase the house and gardens. However, this was only the start, and

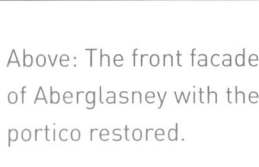

Above: The front facade
of Aberglasney with the
portico restored.

16 years further on, after many long hours of indescribably hard work by a dedicated team, the gardens are again something very special and have once more become truly entrancing for a growing number of visitors.

As part of the restoration work in the garden there was a bold move to bring the yew tunnel back to its former glory. In 1995 there was much dead wood within the structure and new growth was completely shaded out. In 1999 when gardeners started to cut substantial parts of the yews back there were many expressions of concern from people who thought that this might kill the whole thing. However, the process, which was spread over nine years, weeded out dead wood, let in the light and really did reinvigorate the trees, which responded by throwing out plenty of healthy new growth.

Since a lot of the boles are twisted and fused together it is quite difficult to be exact about their number and age. Originally, many tree experts were suggesting an age of perhaps 1,000 years for the tunnel. Today, with the benefit of dendrochronology it has been shown that they are only 280 years old, but it does bring them more vividly to life when one can attribute them to an exact date and the hand that planted them. The tunnel has been formed by training the trees over in an arch, so that the tops meet the ground where they have taken root to form the living tunnel; and yet one wonders if that was always the vision for them in the eighteenth century, or whether a later generation at Aberglasney saw their ornamental potential as the tunnel.

While Aberglasney is truly proud of its rich heritage, to be savoured in the historic elements of its garden revival, it no longer simply heralds itself as 'a garden lost in time'. Instead it is truely 'a garden of past, present and future'.

Ramsey Island Junipers

42 Map A5

From the far western extremity of Pembrokeshire, near St. David's, barely a mile crossing of the turbulent Ramsey Sound brings you to the eastern shores of Ramsey Island. The currents here are strong and on a stormy day the swell can often be too dangerous for boats to make the short journey. Ramsey is owned and managed by the RSPB, with a warden in residence all year round, a life that in winter is sometimes not far removed from that of the old lighthouse keepers.

The island is famed for its remarkable birdlife, attracting a steady stream of ornithologists from far and wide. Breeding birds of spring and summer include guillemots, razorbills, kittiwakes and fulmars, and there are plenty of peregrine falcons, ravens and choughs to be seen on the high cliffs; the presence of the latter species being one of the main reasons why the RSPB originally acquired the site. Until about 10 years ago there was a problem for breeding birds, not just with rats which had originally arrived on shore after swimming from nearby stricken vessels but also the feral cats which had been brought in to deal with the rats. That problem was resolved so that now, as well as the return of Manx shearwaters and storm petrels, there's an ongoing scheme to lure puffins to the island to nest using puffin decoys. It hasn't worked yet, but everyone is hopeful.

While most people will visit to watch the birds, there are other attractions here. There is a glorious flora to enjoy and in the autumn upwards of 400 Atlantic grey seal pups are reared in the coves and caves. However trees do not immediately present themselves as a big feature. Diligent exploration of the cliffs reveals a few stunted trees hanging on as low-lying scrub vegetation – wild privet and blackthorn occurring with some regularity. But, the tree to really try and find here is the juniper – all four specimens!

The first reference to juniper (*Juniperus communis*) on the island appears to come from the early seventeenth century when the Welsh-born composer Thomas Tomkins (1572–1656) paid a visit and remarked upon, 'a great store of juniper' amongst the island's vegetation. From this we must assume that it was then a fairly abundant plant. A late nineteenth-century OS map for the island marks an 'Ogof Juniper' on the east coast, but the first botanist to record juniper here was a Mrs. M. Barnes of St. David's in 1961. Since the 1970s much interest has been shown in these junipers, with an ongoing debate about their status. Three other plants have subsequently been discovered on the mainland coast of Pembrokeshire.

Above: A boat full of visiting naturalists pauses to observe the juniper growing on the eastern cliffs of Ramsey Island as well as some of the Atlantic grey seals currently rearing their pups in the coves.

The Ramsey trees have been compared to other colonies of juniper growing elsewhere in Britain and, typified by their prostrate form, most closely resemble a small colony growing at The Lizard, in Cornwall, a subspecies called *hemisphaerica*. The most interesting aspect of these trees, given their isolated situation, is whether or not they might be a relict population with links back to the post-glacial period some 9,000 years ago. Pollen records gleaned from other parts of Pembrokeshire show that from 11,000 to 12,000 years ago juniper, Scots pine, willows and birch were all in evidence, but there have not been any other studies of more recent peat bog deposits to confirm its presence after the last Ice Age. Juniper does not respond well to shading so, as Britain warmed the rampant colonization of trees such as birch and hazel would have seen a diminishing presence for the juniper; the best refuges where the tree might survive being the sort of sea-cliff habitats where it still clings on. Undoubtedly these little trees on Ramsey have some great age, perhaps several hundred years – something which is remarkable in itself. However establishing their true lineage is currently a matter for conjecture.

An alternative explanation for the presence of these junipers could be so much simpler. If similar trees are found in Cornwall then it brings into question the potential role of migratory birds that might have consumed the berries, carrying them northwards before depositing them in some cliff-top hollow where they alighted to roost.

The Bleeding Yew
of Nevern

43 Map B5

Little more than a couple of miles inland from the delights of the Pembrokeshire coast, just above Newport, lies the village of Nevern, with its fine Norman church of St. Brynach poised above a bend in the river Nevern. The squat, square, castellated tower is actually the only remnant of the original Norman church, but this has been a site of ecclesiastical importance since the sixth century.

On entering the churchyard a short path, deeply shaded by an avenue of eight yew trees, leads to the church door. Old yew avenues are not a particularly common feature, so these contorted, entwined trees, generally considered to be in the region of 600 years old, are special in their own right. However, one tree in particular, the second on the right hand side, has been famed for many years as 'the bleeding yew'; for a sticky, red, blood-like fluid exudes from a wound where a bough was cut away in the nineteenth century. There are also one or two other small orifices in the trunk that weep in this way.

Understandably, this weird phenomenon has led to various local lores and legends. Christian believers have long held that the tree weeps for the crucifixion of Christ, the wounds of the tree symbolising where his limbs were nailed to the cross. Pagan believers, on the other hand, see a vision of the earth mother in the tree, the bleeding redolent of menstruation. It is said that a man, possibly a monk, was hanged from the tree (his crime unknown), but protesting his innocence he cried out, 'If you hang me guiltless as I am, these trees will bleed for me.' Another variation of the theme recounts the tale of a condemned man who had his hand cut off for some violation of the forest law. Either way, such barbaric events conjure scenes of much greater antiquity than the nineteenth century when the 'bleeding' appears to have begun. The first reference to this tree, according to the Ancient Yew Group, is to be found in George Nicholson's *The Cambrian Traveller's Guide* of 1840. Discovering earlier written records of this phenomenon in association with accompanying folklore or, better still, factual events prior to the nineteenth century could prove even more fascinating.

'...a sticky, red, blood-like fluid exudes from a wound where a bough was cut away in the nineteenth century.'

Various observers have offered far more mundane explanations of this occurrence. It is thought that rainwater along with by-products of decaying detritus within the hollow trunk have become stained by the red heartwood. This fluid then finds a point of egress, with the colonisation by wild yeasts turning it into the thick blood-like fluid.

Near the yews stands one of the finest Celtic crosses in Wales, dating from the tenth or early eleventh century. Carved from the local dolerite stone, it is richly decorated with wonderful braided designs. Elsewhere in the churchyard, discover the fine row of 26 Irish yews (*Taxus baccata* 'Fastigiata'), planted in 1928 to the memory of those members of the parish who perished in the Great War.

Laburnum Hedges
of Ceredigion

44 Map B5

A trip through Ceredigion in May or early June, depending on how advanced the spring might be, brings the reward of one of the finest hedgerow scenes that Britain has to offer; although the first week of May 2011 revealed a stunning and earlier than usual flowering of the laburnum hedges. The occurrence of these strange hedges may be widespread within the county, but the triangle formed between Synod Inn, along the A487 to Brynhoffnant, and south to Penrhiw-pâl seems to produce the greatest concentration of this most unusual and unfathomable countryside feature.

'...this most unusual and unfathomable countryside feature.'

Laburnums are native to southern Europe and western Asia, and arrived in Britain in the latter half of the sixteenth century. There are two principal species – common laburnum (*Laburnum anagroides*), which accounts for the majority of the Ceredigion trees, and Scotch laburnum (*Laburnum alpinum*), this latter species being absent from these hedges, although the hybrid form – *Laburnum x watereri* 'Vossii'– accounts for about 10 per cent of the hedgerow trees. The hybrid has probably been planted to extend the flowering season of the hedges (it flowers slightly later), but some trees may have been incidental occurrences where common laburnum has crossed with garden specimens of Scotch laburnum.

Driving through the countryside spotting all these hedges begs the question as to why on earth would a tree like laburnum, with its known toxicity, be planted around field margins where it can be grazed by livestock. The greatest concentrations of the toxic compound citisine are evident in the bark and seeds, which accounts for the fears over children eating the seed pods (which resemble small pea pods) and suffering acute gastric conditions. Despite its bad reputation, records of death from ingestion are virtually unknown. Sheep, cattle and horses have been observed to eat the foliage with impunity. As a stock-proof hedging plant laburnum seems a poor choice, as its natural

'Most of the laburnum hedges are adjudged to have been planted during the first half of the nineteenth century...'

Above: A superb laburnum hedge near the village of Pentregat – one of the best places to see an abundance of these singular hedges.

propensity is to grow straight up rather than bushing out at the base, particularly after coppicing, and the tree does not respond well to laying.

Most of the laburnum hedges are adjudged to have been planted during the first half of the nineteenth century, but reference material from the period gives few if any clues to the reasons for planting. J.C. Loudon, in his *Arboretum et Fruticetum Britannicum* of 1838, lists several uses for the timber which he cites as the most valuable of all timbers grown in Scotland, and his introduction to the tree's synonyms raises interesting possibilities. Bean-trefoile Tree, Peascod Tree (Gerard) and Golden Chain were obviously derived from the trefoil leaves, the long golden racemes and the pea-like seed pods. However, 'The [name] Arbois is a corruption of *arc-bois* [literally, bow wood], the wood of this tree

Above: An impressive laburnum hedge near Llanwnnen.
Right: A huge laburnum hedge along an old hedge bank near Plwmp. Clearly these trees have been coppiced in the past, but not for a long time.

having been used by the ancient Gauls to make their bows; and still so employed by the country people, in some parts of the Macon-nois, where these bows are found to preserve their strength and elasticity during half a century.' An Act passed in the reign of Edward IV enjoined every Englishman to have a bow of his own height made of, 'yew, wych-hazel [most probably wych elm], ash or awburne,' the latter being laburnum.

The wood of laburnum is indeed extremely durable and also turns well; the heart wood being a deep chocolate brown while the sap wood is a contrasting honey-yellow colour. Loudon continues with his list of uses, 'it is also used for the bowls of punch-ladles; for flutes, and other musical instruments; for knife handles, pegs and wedges; and for pulleys and blocks.' It was also much in

demand by cabinet makers for inlays and veneers, as well as being used as faux-ebony for the handles of teapots. It is reputed that laburnum staves were once used as fence posts and that the tree's ability to strike roots easily may have led to these developing into hedge trees.

Some recent observers have simply deduced that these colourful hedges were planted as a vernacular response to the highly ornamented parks and gardens of the gentry, who undoubtedly employed laburnum amongst their grand schemes. It is fine to conjecture, but perhaps the mystery of the laburnum hedges is just part of their allure.

'...the heart wood being a deep chocolate brown while the sap wood is a contrasting honey-yellow colour.'

Strata Florida Yews

45 Map C4

The last resting place of one of Wales' most celebrated literary sons has made the peaceful retreat of the Cistercian Abbey of Strata Florida, founded in 1184 by Rhys ap Gruffyd, a place of pilgrimage for many centuries; not just for religious devotions but also in celebration of Dafydd ap Gwilym (c.1320–c.1380), the renowned medieval poet, who is said to be interred beneath one of the yew trees in the churchyard. During his lifetime it is known that Strata Florida was something of a cultural and literary focal point, which would seem to add credence to his burial here.

Today there are only two yew trees left in the churchyard, but the earliest reference to yews growing here comes from John Leland, during his travels in the mid-sixteenth century. In fact these were the only yews on his travels that he was moved to remark upon, so they must have been rather special. Leland wrote:

'The church of Strateflere is larg, side ilid abd cross ilid; by is a large cloister. The fratry and infirmitory be now mere ruines. The foundation of the body of the church was made to have bene 60 foote longer than it is now. The coemiteri wherein the cunteri about doth buri is very large, and meanly waullid with stone. In it be xxxix great hue trees. The base court or camp afore the abbey is very fair and large.'

If the number of accounts and engravings of the abbey from the eighteenth century onwards are anything to go by, Strata Florida has long been an essential destination for pilgrims and tourists alike, but most of the 39 yews were long gone before the nineteenth century. The writer George Borrow, visiting in 1854, mentions two yews growing in the churchyard, but strangely, by 1874, the Worcestershire botanist Edwin Lees visited the site and remarked upon three yew trees in the churchyard. An engraving from the *Gardener's Chronicle* of that year shows a ruinous yew with a huge void through the middle – a tree that seems to have disappeared by the turn of the nineteenth century.

Of the two yews that survive in the churchyard, one is a craggy old female tree close to the chapel, set about with a plinth of stones. Popular belief acclaims this tree as the one under which Dafydd ap Gwilym is buried, but this is a comparatively recent tradition. In 1951 members of the Honourable Society of the Cymmrodorion gathered around this tree to erect a small memorial stone to Dafydd ap Gwilym. After all, of the two trees present this was the biggest, with its girth of 23 feet (7 metres), and must have looked the part for such a ceremony. A translation of a poem by one of Dafydd's contemporaries,

Above: The female yew assumed to be the 'Dafydd Tree' since 1951. Top right: Memorials to Dafydd ap Gwilym beneath the female yew tree in the churchyard at Strata Florida Abbey.

Gruffyd Gryg, was read out by Professor T.H. Parry-Williams; the first four lines of which are highly illuminating:

> At Ystrad Fflur, beside the hall,
> There grows a yew against the wall.
> God bless this yew for whom 'tis bliss
> To be the house where Dafydd is;

The clue is in the second line. The female tree is not close to any structure, but the smaller, male tree, about 200 feet to the north-east of the female, is close to the northern perimeter wall of the churchyard. Further investigation of this tree reveals that it is the partial remains of a much bigger tree. George Borrow (who knew of the Gryg poem) was of the opinion in 1854 that this was the 'Dafydd Tree" and also mentions that it appeared to have been struck by

lightning or storm damaged so that a large part of it had died and fallen away. The conclusion is that both surviving trees were probably once roughly the same size and vintage; around 1,500 years old. Robert Bevan-Jones in his book *The Ancient Yew* has done exhaustive research and also feels sure that this is the true 'Dafydd Tree'; an opinion reinforced by a 1920s postcard which names it as such.

The ultimate truth is that we will never know for sure, for the poet could have been buried beneath any of the 39 yews that Leland found, although one suspects that Dafydd ap Gwilym's enduring significance to the historic culture and literature of Wales should have ensured that his own special tree would have been most carefully preserved. Today this is a place of overwhelming tranquillity, with only the gurgle of the nearby infant Teifi and the distant bleating of sheep to break the peace. The spirit of the poet still roams this gentle valley.

Ystrad Meurig Ash

46 Map C4

Ash trees don't often figure in the leagues of ancient or remarkable broadleaf trees, largely because they seldom achieve any great age or size when compared to the likes of oaks or sweet chestnuts. 200 years old is quite exceptional for the species. If anything the oldest trees will almost certainly be coppice stools, and often these are found in woods or hedgerows.

So discovering an ash tree that defies all the norms of the species is something of real note. In the little village of Ystrad Meurig in Ceredigion grows a tree that seems to have survived in a most unusual form. First inspection from the roadside reveals a bole that appears to have a very broad base with numerous branches of fairly recent growth ascending vertically – seemingly a coppice stool. However, once around the other side, the sprawling, buttressed base of the tree forms a giant ring around a great void where the centre of the tree once grew. The sense is of an old maiden, or perhaps a pollard, which has rotted away inside while the live sapwood around the outer edge has continued to carry the tree onward and upward. The girth measures almost 23 feet (7 metres) around – outstanding dimensions for any ash and surely making it one of the largest in Wales.

The vitality of the sapwood is indisputable, its new growth enfolding the dead carcass of the inner tree and a healthy growth of poles shooting skyward, so that one can only assume that regular lopping has been the secret of this tree's longevity (although the farmer who owns the tree can't remember when it was last cut). Inside the central cavity strange and slightly spooky anthropomorphic beasts and faces can be delineated in the rotting hardwood.

Hafod Beeches

47 Map C4

Right: An artist sits and sketches beside the Nant Gau as it cuts down through the limestone of the Hafod Estate.

Aberystwyth, on the west coast of Wales, has been a popular resort since Victorian times, but there is a remarkable place that verges on a well-kept secret, nestled in the Ystwyth valley some 12 miles inland, which very few people know about. The Hafod Estate or, to give it its full name, Hafod Uchtryd is one of best remaining examples of a late eighteenth- century 'picturesque' landscape in Europe.

One of the most influential landscape theorists was the cleric, schoolmaster and amateur artist Rev. William Gilpin (1724–1804) who made a series of tours around the countryside of Britain, painting and recording his thoughts about the various elements of both the natural topography and the architectural heritage. Distillations of his travels were later published (from 1782 onwards) in a series of books in which he promulgated his formulation of the 'picturesque'; by definition, expressive of that peculiar kind of beauty which is agreeable in a picture". Gilpin's views might have originally been for the benefit of artists, but no sooner were they published than landscape fashion took flight, with many landscapers eager to offer their services and wealthy landowners able to set the new schemes in motion.

Thomas Johnes (1748–1816) inherited the estate at Hafod in 1780 and was so appalled by both its dereliction and the dismal conditions for the estate workers that he set forth to build not only a fine house and gardens but also a productive estate in both forestry and agriculture, thus providing employment and better habitation for the estate staff. Johnes was hugely influenced by

Above: The impressive Hafod Beech, hidden away on top of Allt Dihanog.

William Gilpin's 'picturesque' movement and contrived a network of scenic paths and views across much of the estate. Yet he was no dilettante romantic. Welsh woodland historian, Dr. William Linnard, has no doubt that Johnes was the greatest ever tree planter in Wales, since he oversaw the planting of around five million trees, amounting to some 1,000–1,200 acres, between 1782 and 1816. No mean feat.

The whole estate fell into neglect during the twentieth century and for reasons of safety the old mansion was demolished in 1958. However, in 1987 the Friends of Hafod was established, and soon an alliance with both the Welsh Historic Gardens Trust and Forestry Commission Wales saw the creation of the Hafod Trust in 1994. Since this time a steady process of restoration has brought the beauty of the old estate back to life.

In his time Johnes may have been a great planter of conifers – more than half the trees he planted were larch – but he was also a great fan of broadleaf trees, and beech in particular. Near the site of the old house several massive beeches with vast moss-clad roots grip the hillsides, and at Pant Melyn, on the Gentleman's Walk, there are some very handsome beeches that are easily big enough to have been planted by Johnes 200 years ago.

Above:"Cascade above the Mossy Seat", a plate from "Fifteen Views Illustrative of a Tour to Havod in Cardiganshire", 1810. Produced from a series of original watercolour drawings by John 'Warwick' Smith (1749–1831). The Hafod Beech sits high above this scene to the right of the picture.

However, one of the most spectacular beech trees to be found on the estate is actually hidden away on the wooded hilltop of Allt Dihanog to the south of the site of the old house. It takes a bit of scrambling and good fortune to finally locate the tree, but the struggle is well worth it. The Hafod Beech is a truly remarkable and phenomenally large-girthed tree, measuring a majestic 27 feet 9 inches (8.46 metres) around. It has the appearance of either an outgrown coppice stool or perhaps a short and neglected pollard – it certainly could be either, and yet some observers believe that this could be an example of a bundle-planted beech tree. This would indicate that several saplings were popped in the same planting hole and allowed to grow up in such close confines that the stems have all become fused together to create the impression of a single tree. There are no historic records of this type of intentional planting ever occurring, but perhaps one of Johnes' foresters simply did it as an experiment, or maybe the saplings were heeled in after a busy day's planting because the forester was tired and hungry and intended to plant them out properly at a later date; although he never returned. There is even a possibility that Johnes directed such a planting, wishing to create a unique feature for the parkland landscape, for it would once have been visible from the house. It is all pure conjecture, but it does add to the intrigue of this most singular and impressive tree.

Prostrate Blackthorn

48 Map C4

Blackthorn (*Prunus spinosa*) is a tree seldom regarded as being of much significance as an isolated or prime specimen tree, and it is more often found as a constituent species in hedgerows where its dense and spiny growth make it ideally suited for effective stockproof barriers. In the autumn the tongue-curlingly astringent fruits are keenly sought by makers of sloe gin who are happy to battle with the tree's devilish thorns for their prize. Caution must me exercised not to be pierced by a thorn or get it lodged in a skin puncture as wounds are highly prone to turning septic. On the odd occasion that a blackthorn tree is allowed to grow into a mature tree it becomes a very handsome individual, particularly in early spring when it is decked in purest white blossom. Flowering in early April the tree makes a useful early source of nectar for bees.

Whether it is viewed as a vice or a virtue, blackthorn has the capacity for rampant suckering. If this bolsters the density of a hedgerow then clearly this is a virtue, but often the suckers will ramble into abandoned or under-grazed pastures where their thorns can become a serious hazard for livestock or even tractor tyres. Blackthorn has enormously varied habits and morphology and appears to be very salt tolerant, so perhaps it should not be surprising to find a remarkable specimen growing in a bare shingle beach, just a few yards from the tideline near Aberystwyth.

Small, prostrate examples of blackthorn are not infrequent along the coast of Wales, but on the landward side of Tanybwlch beach grows a tree of great size and antiquity. The most impressive aspect of its size is the area of ground that this one tree has managed to cover in a seemingly adverse environment. Local botanist Arthur Chater has been monitoring the tree's progress for many years and his research has uncovered documentation dating back more than a century. A photograph taken in 1910 shows the tree (or perhaps trees, as they were then understood) looking much as it does today. The photographer, botanist Richard Henry Yapp, considered the tree(s) to be, 'of considerable age, probably not much less than a century old'. In 1935 John Henry Salter also observed that they were, 'probably of great age'. In 1938 and 1939 Salter reported that violent storms had killed much of the blackthorn here. However, Chater records that in 1979 some 20 patches of the tree covered an area 49 x 20 feet (15 x 6 metres), and by 2001 around 55 patches of the tree were now growing in an area 88 x 33 feet (27 x 10 metres).

'...the tongue-curlingly astringent fruits are keenly sought by makers of sloe gin...'

Above: Part of the extensive prostrate blackthorn that rambles across Tanybwlch beach near Aberystwyth.

In 2001, in a bid to gain a clearer picture of exactly how this tree was composed, Cresswell and Hayes used DNA fingerprinting on nine patches of the tree from the extremities of its perceived territory, as well as comparative samples from seven nearby blackthorns. Remarkably, all nine samples were the same and distinct from their sampled neighbours. This establishes that the patches are, at the very least, clonally identical, but whether they all still have a common root system, are suckers which have latterly become independent or are even the tips of a deeply buried tree is a conundrum that has yet to be solved. However it is viewed, the little clumps of this 200-year-old tree appear like a wonderful, random, alpine garden amongst the sea-washed shingle. Be careful how you step.

Petrified Forest at Borth

49 Map C4

When neap tides leave the foreshore to the north of Borth exposed hundreds of lumps and bumps may be seen poking through the wet sand. These are not boulders, but sea-sculpted tree stumps. Pull away the seaweed and the annual rings of the tree trunks are still clearly visible. Known as the 'Petrified Forest', most of these stumps are still very much wood rather than stone (like fossils) as they have been well preserved in the anaerobic conditions beneath the sea.

Right: 6,000 year old pieces of birch in the sands at Borth are still clearly recognisable. Left: View southward along the beach towards Borth.

'These are not boulders, but sea-sculpted tree stumps.'

Oak, hazel, birch and willow have been identified but most of the trees have been found to be Scots pines and have been dated to a period around 5,000–6,000 years ago when glacial melt water filled the basin between Ireland and Wales. Scots pine has not been regarded as a native species in Wales since climate warming caused its native range to move northward, so that today true native Scots pines can only be found in Scotland. William Linnard has studied historic accounts, Welsh folklore and pollen analysis to conclude in his *Welsh Woods and Forests* that these petrified pines are the last of the natives.

The melting of the ice sheets, which covered Scotland to a depth of about three kilometres some 20,000 years ago, has had a longstanding effect on the land mass of Britain, causing post-glacial rebound. Effectively, with the relief from the weight of ice, northern Britain has risen while there has been a gradual downward tilting of the land mass in southern Britain. This would also have been a contributory factor to the submerging of the Borth forest. Coastal water levels are still rising around southern Britain as the tilt continues, giving rise to fears of future flooding in areas such as the lower Thames Valley.

A more lyrical explanation for the 'Petrified Forest' has filtered down through Welsh folklore. It is said that once upon a time there was a land called Cantre'r Gwaelod (The Lowland Hundred) off the coast here – villages and farms aplenty protected by a great dyke to ward off the dangerous high tides.

'Some say that on stormy nights the bells from the submerged church can still be heard.'

Above: View northward along the beach towards Ynyslas.
Left: Bizarre tree-like images have been left, etched in the sand near this ancient stump, in the wake of the ebbing tide.

When floodwaters threatened it was the job of one Seithenhin, the designated watchman, to close the great gates of the dyke. One day he got exceedingly drunk, some say he was lovelorn, and neglected his duties. The sea flooded in and Cantre'r Gwaelod was flooded for evermore. Some say that on stormy nights the bells from the submerged church can still be heard.

Borth may be the best known of Wales' petrified forests but it is by no means the only site; always bearing in mind that extremely low tides (usually spring and autumn) provide the best chances of seeing these remarkable features. Worth a look are Penmaenmawr, below Conwy on the north coast; sites to the north of Borth such as Tywyn; several sites around the southern coastline of Pembrokeshire and Carmarthen Bay, of which Amroth is perhaps best known; off the Mumbles and at Goldcliff, just south of Newport, Monmouthshire. It must be said that tides do run very swiftly across these sites so do keep a weather eye on conditions so that you don't get into difficulties.

Mallwyd Yew

50 Map C3

The little village of Mallwyd lies at the most southerly end of the county of Gwynedd, right on the old boundaries between Montgomeryshire and Merionethshire, and set within the Dyfi Valley. As Samuel Lewis described it in 1833, 'The village is delightfully situated in a small but fertile valley, watered by the Dovey [Dyfi], and abounding with finely diversified and highly picturesque scenery, formed by the various indentations of the three lofty mountains of Aran, Camlan, and Moeldyvi, which surround it like an amphitheatre.'

Today it appears to most travellers as merely a major junction between the A470 and the A458, but it must have been this ancient crossing of two major routes that led to the establishment of the nearby village. There has been a church here since the sixth century, dedicated to St. Tydecho, but the present incarnation is a fourteenth-century building.

The first mention of the yews at Mallwyd is to be found in Thomas Pennant's *The Tour in North Wales* in 1783, when he was moved to relate that, 'One of the beautiful yew trees in the church yard, is extremely well worth notice. It is a sort of forest of vast trees, issuing from one stem, forming a most extensive shade, and magnificent appearance.'

Perhaps spurred by Pennant's account, Reverend Richard Warner, in his *A Second walk through Wales* from 1798, was, 'induced to stroll into the churchyard, remarkable for several enormous yew trees, of which 4 measure 15 feet, and one 27 feet in circumference.' These trees were sufficiently impressive to merit several further mentions throughout the nineteenth century. A splendid account may be found in The *Monthly magazine or British register* (Vol.39) for 1815:

'In the church-yard of Mallwyd, is a yew-tree, that, tradition says, is 700 years old; and it is not easy to imagine a spot where a yew-tree could have witnessed fewer vicissitudes in the objects around, during that length of time, The rivers, the rocks, and the mountains, are immutable, The woods are the lineal descendants of those that flourished when the yew was planted. The houses, probably, differ little in number, and but few of them in convenience. The roads are undoubtedly the same; for no-where else could they be made to pass: they are only widened to admit a carriage. The yew-tree has nine distinct trunks, one in the centre, and eight that surround it; and the circumference of their united branches is computed at upwards of 200 feet.'

Samuel Lewis remarks upon the yews in his *Topographical Dictionary of Wales* in 1833, 'In the churchyard are three remarkably fine yew trees, one of which measures 28 feet 3 inches in girth, and from one stem throws out a great number of scions, which spread around it an extensive shade, and together present an appearance of sombre magnificence.'

This description truly befits the greatest specimen which still dominates the south-east corner of the churchyard today, although some of those lesser trees mentioned by Warner have gone. The biggest yew, a male, still exists as a multi-stemmed tree, although it would appear that the central stem may well have developed from an aerial root. There is evidence of some remnant parts of the original outer bole and some of the multiple stems may be fragmented parts of this. The tree has a girth of 33 feet (10 metres) at 3 feet above ground, which might be seen as quite a large increment of growth since 1833, however there is every chance that Lewis's measurement was made at ground level, which may account for the disparity.

Lone Yew of Llynierth

51 Map C3

At the southern end of Bala Lake a strange and seemingly unexplainable small circular mound lies close to the shoreline. Atop the mound stands, or rather kneels, a decrepit old yew tree, heeling over at an alarming angle with its knotted and gnarled root system partially wrenched from the earth, and yet the old tree is still very much alive. Several observers have mused on the significance of this odd little mound with its signal tree, one obvious conclusion is that it might be some ancient ceremonial or burial site by the lake edge. However, recent research has dispelled such spiritual if not romantic notions.

Above / right: Upturned roots of the Lone Yew of Llynierth at the southern end of Bala Lake.

Opposite the yew and its mound stands the fine old mansion of Glan-llyn. Now an outdoor pursuits centre, this was once the summer shooting lodge for the Williams-Wynn family of Wynnstay, near Ruabon (see also the Queen's Oak p.25). During the nineteenth century they were one of the largest landowners and most powerful and influential families in Wales; a reputation reinforced by a *Punch* cartoon of the period showing Sir Watkin Williams-Wynn (1820–1885) boldly entitled 'The Prince IN Wales' with the additional text – "I am monarch of all I survey, my right there is none to dispute". A similar cartoon from *Vanity Fair* in 1873 lauds him as "The King of Wales."

Recent correspondence received from Penri Jones, who lives nearby, reveals that many years ago he was told by his father that the mound on which the yew stands was constructed as a safe haven and nesting site for swans and, indeed, the site has been commonly known throughout living memory as '*Ynys yr Alarch*' (Swan Island). Having ones own swannery would undoubtedly have been regarded as a highly prestigious symbol amongst the gentry and, by the sound of it, this would have sat very well with Sir Watkin Williams-Wynn.

Until the 1950s the lake had a much higher water level than it does today, since it was substantially lowered by the Dee Regulation Scheme of 1953–4, so that other than at times of flood the island is now high and dry. However, a good impression of the original purpose of the site may be gleaned, with the higher ground for the safety of the swans along with the protective, surrounding moat to ward off any predators. Yews were implemented as part of the landscaping of the grounds of Glan-llyn, so Penri Jones believes that a yew tree on the island was merely an extension of this scheme, drawing attention to a wealthy man's declaration of status as well as being an ideal tree for year round shelter for the swans. Sadly, swans no longer dwell here, but it would be fascinating to know when this little island was last a safe haven for these beautiful birds.

Llanddeiniolen Yews

52 Map C2

The majority of Wales' most celebrated and ancient yew trees seem to occur through the border counties, with Herefordshire and Shropshire similarly containing a respectable array of these remarkable old trees; so it is with some surprise to discover the churchyard of St. Deiniolen, in the tiny hamlet of Llanddeiniolen near Caernarfon, containing three massive yews of gargantuan proportions. Hollowed, split and sprawling above the sharply defined, slate-slabbed table tombs, these rugged old bystanders must surely have signalled a site of sanctity for around the last 2,000 years.

It is believed that the site was first established as a 'cell' by St. Deiniolen around AD 580, while other sources cite the establishment of the first church here to AD 616. There are natural springs close by; a presence which frequently corroborates an early saint cell. One, mentioned by Samuel Lewis in 1833, 'about a mile south of the church is Fynnon Deiniolen, or St. Deiniolen's Well, the water of which was formerly held in high esteem for its efficacy in the cure of rheumatic and scorbutic diseases.' The connection between ancient yews as landmarks for springs and wells and, by association, religious focal points, is widespread and well documented. There have been several generations of buildings here, but the church today dates from the 1840s.

About 200 years ago travellers and writers began to investigate and document every nook and cranny of Britain's topography. Earliest mentions of the Llanddeiniolen yews come from *A Description of Caernarvonshire* (1809/11) by E. Hyde Hall, who found, 'several yew trees, bald and ragged with antiquity,' and Richard Fenton in his *Tours in Wales* (1810) also, 'visited Llanddeiniolen church. The largest yew trees I ever saw of so fantastick a growth.'

Before long, some of the nineteenth-century visitors were moved to actually record the dimensions of the yews, which makes interesting comparisons to current dimensions, although we have no information about exactly where on the trees' boles the measurements were taken. In Samuel Lewis's *A Topographical Dictionary of Wales* (1833) he notes that, 'in the churchyard are several yew trees, of luxuriant growth [a description seemingly at variance with that of Hyde Hall – *see above*], one of which measures twenty-eight feet four inches in girth.' By 1865 this largest tree of the three, a female to the left of the approach path, was then recorded as, 'nearly 30 feet in girth.'

Recent measurements, a little above ground level, reveal almost exactly the same girth, so virtually no growth in the last 145 years. Maybe this is one of those periods of stasis for which ancient yews are renowned – a strange phenomenon which continues to wreathe the growth mode of the yew in mystery.

In the early twentieth century the academic, poet, writer and politician William John Gruffydd (1881–1954) was moved to write one of his most famous poems about the greatest yew tree here – 'Ywen Llanddeiniolen.'

Bodnant
Laburnum Arch

Above: View from the upper terrace at Bodnant, with a glimpse of the River Conwy in the distance and the mountains of Snowdonia beyond.

Left: Dilapidated hybrid strawberry tree on the terrace. Almost every visitor who passes this strange and sensuous form seems compelled to give it a little stroke.

'A single day is simply not long enough to explore and absorb such a splendid garden.'

There are enough photographs available online and in print to give any potential visitor to Bodnant Gardens, near Conwy, a pretty good overview of the horticultural treats that lie in wait, but the reality is miles better by far. A single day is simply not long enough to explore and absorb such a splendid garden.

Bodnant is a garden principally established during the late ninteenth and early twentieth centuries, initially by Henry Davis Pochin from 1874 and, subsequently, through the marriage of his daughter, by the McLaren family. Bodnant Hall was originally built in 1792, although Pochin carried out much remodelling, so that it now has the presence of a Victorian country house.

With 80 acres of ground as his palette, Pochin engaged the landscape architect Edward Milner to realise his vision, digging pools, building terraces and planting a wonderful variety of exotic trees from all over the world. These have responded brilliantly to the damp and protected conditions, particularly in the deep valley called The Dell. The Tree Register reveals that there are a dozen champion trees in this garden, but the feature for which Bodnant is justly most famous has to be the sensational Laburnum Arch – probably the finest of its type in the world.

During the early 1880s Pochin and Milner devised their laburnum arch at the top of the garden, just inside the eastern perimeter wall. A gently arching tunnel some 180 feet long was densely planted on either side with Voss's laburnum (*Laburnum x watereri*), a hybrid between common laburnum (*Laburnum anagyroides*) and Scotch laburnum (*Laburnum alpinum*), which produces later flowering, vivid yellow racemes of greater length than either of the two parent species. An exterior backdrop of vibrant pinks and soft oranges of azaleas completes the picture. It is a captivating experience to linger beneath the tumbling cascades of gold, inhaling the pungent scent of the flowers, lulled by the gentle drone of a thousand bees.

Closer inspection of the size of many of the individual trees that make up the arch leads to a reassessment of its actual vintage. Some trees are clearly very recent replacements and, in fact, the oldest trees are little more than thirty years old. So, while the feature of the Laburnum Arch can justifiably claim its Victorian roots, the current manifestation is relatively young. A conversation with Troy Smith, the current head gardener, revealed that there have been perennial problems with poor drainage around the trees as well as salt run-off leaching through the soil from the road just a few feet above, which has probably adversely affected the laburnums in the past. Measures are now in place to ameliorate these issues so a brighter future and longer lifespan hopefully awaits the present trees of this far-famed arch.

Llangernyw Yew

54 Map C2

For many years the residents of Llangernyw, a little village in the county of Conwy, knew that they had a fine old yew tree in their churchyard, but little realising that it was amongst the largest and oldest trees in Wales. In 1995 Jon Stokes and Kevin Hand of The Tree Council happened to be in the area, running a training day for Tree Wardens, when they visited the village for the first time. Walking into the churchyard of St. Digain they were astounded to find a monstrous ancient yew that had previously been completely unknown to all tree experts, writers and yew enthusiasts. There is no mention of the tree in any of the nineteenth century tree books, including John Lowe's comprehensive *The Yew Trees of Great Britain and Ireland* of 1897, or later on in Vaughan Cornish's *The Churchyard Yew and Immortality* of 1946, where a long list of remarkable Welsh yew trees are listed.

Looking at the tree today it would appear to be in the best of health, but back in 1995 it was under no little threat by the presence of a large oil tank, installed

to feed the church's heating system, wedged fair and square in the middle of the splayed shell of the great bole. The Tree Council arranged for the tank's removal and, as part of National Tree Week celebrations, a memorial stone in honour of this 'Green Monument' was erected in the churchyard and unveiled on 25 November.

Clearly this remarkable male yew tree has some serious antiquity, and a measurement around the tree back in 1995 soon confirmed this – initially, 36 feet (11 metres) made it arguably the largest yew in Wales at the time although subsequent measurements, allowing for one partially prone section of the tree, have come out at a little over 34 feet (10.4 metres). That is the problem with accurately measuring such old giants. Different results frequently occur depending upon the exact point of measurement. Current thinking is that the 37 feet (11.3 metres) of the Discoed Yew in Powys pips this tree to being the largest and oldest in Wales but this is mere detail, for undoubtedly the tree is ancient.

Here again controversy attends the exact estimation of age. At one extreme the Conservation Foundation's Yew Tree Campaign certified that the tree was 4,000–5,000 years old. Conversely, Robert Bevan-Jones, in his book *The Ancient Yew* (2003), argues against such exaggerated estimates through his belief that these trees were planted in association with early saint cells (St. Digain hailing from the fifth century), rather than the earlier pagan connections often attributed to these ancient yews This would make the tree no more than 1,500 years old. Thus a huge disparity exists, based on a mixture of different beliefs, suppositions and extrapolation from the known ages of recorded trees, but ultimately one that is difficult to rationalise, since yews such as this one have lost all their central core of heartwood that held the secret to their true age.

Nantglyn Yew

55 Map D2

Amid the rolling hills of Denbighshire lies the little hamlet of Nantglyn, with its modest and much rebuilt and restored church dedicated to St. James, dating largely from the eighteenth and nineteenth centuries. Records show that there has been a church on this site for about the last 700 years, and there are also vague references to the presence close by of St. Mordeyrn, with his chapel and well, during the sixth century. As in so many other parts of Wales a saint cell is often promulgated by the accompanying presence of an ancient yew tree, and with a girth of 27 feet 3 inches (8.3 metres), the largest yew tree here should be in the region of 1,500 years old, which would bear out the association.

The Nantglyn Yew, or Pulpit Yew, is a fascinating collaboration of ancient tree and architecture, for the hollowed trunk contains a flight of slate steps leading up to a raised seat and podium – a splendid vantage point and natural pulpit. Local legend relates that John Wesley (1703–1791) once visited and preached from this natural pulpit, however there are those that think it unlikely that the great founder of Methodism would have been allowed to hold forth in an Anglican churchyard.

'...a fascinating collaboration of ancient tree and architecture...'

Early accounts of the tree are scant, and nobody knows for sure when the steps were actually installed, but a visitor in the 1850s left a brief observation revealing that the deed had already been done by then. They wrote, '...there has been an aperture on one side of this tree, which is now built up with lime, and stone, and forms a sort of arm chair, raised high out of it, where an active party may climb and sit and view the beauties of the pretty little Vale.' The verdant canopy of this great old tree is in excellent condition and obtaining a clear view of anything much more than the immediate churchyard below is now well-nigh impossible. On the day I chose to photograph the tree all was peaceful until a handsome male song thrush began to flutter about nearby, seemingly chastising me for invading his domain. It wasn't until I edited my photographs later that I discovered the reason for his agitation. In a tiny hole above the ruddy-fluted bole of the tree sat a small-mossy nest and, peeking above the edge, the beady eyes of his mate staring right back at me.

Three Sisters
Sweet Chestnuts

56 Map D2

As the nearby traffic hurtles along the busy A525 between Ruthin and Denbigh, barely any of those speeding travellers would have an inkling of the splendid, ancient Spanish or sweet chestnut (*Castanea sativa*) which stands only a few yards away at the end of a pretty garden which, in former times, belonged to the nearby estate of Bachymbyd.

The house is called 'The Three Sisters' in deference to the three massive sweet chestnuts of the same name that once all thrived close by. Sadly, of the three, only one tree remains. One tree was felled in the nineteenth century and another was later wind thrown; its bleached carcass still recumbent beside its surviving sister. It is popularly believed that these chestnuts were planted by Sir Charles Salusbury in 1670, when his only surviving daughter Jane married Sir Walter Bagot, as a token of the affection that his three daughters held for each other (and probably his affection for them too). It seems uncanny how prophetic the fate of the three sisters has proved to be for the fortunes of the three chestnuts.

'An age of 450 years old puts it firmly in Spanish Armada territory...'

The Three Sisters were already a well-known arboreal landmark by the late eighteenth century when the celebrated traveller, naturalist, antiquarian and author Thomas Pennant observed in his *A Tour in Wales* in 1781, that these were 'fine chestnut trees, one of which is near 24 feet in circumference.' This statistic draws the trees into a debate about their true age. A chestnut tree that had achieved such an impressive girth after only a little over a century seems somewhat unlikely, and one might suspect that its true age then was more like 200 years old. This takes the date of planting back to the mid-sixteenth century. The girth of the surviving tree today is about 42 feet (12.8 metres) give or take a few inches either way because of all the burring, which, when compared to other chestnuts with a known age could make it at least 450 years old ... and possibly a little older than that. An age of 450 years puts it firmly in Spanish Armada territory and the apocryphal stories of chestnuts

plundered from the vanquished Armada only to be planted as a victory proclamation on estates across Britain (see Llanvihangel Court, Monmouthshire p.50).

It is unlikely that we will ever know the true age of this ancient chestnut, for its bole is a hollow shell which fortunately appears to have survived a fire at some point in the past. The tree has clearly been pollarded down the years (although not for some time), but much of the crown is now shattered and dead. No matter, vigorous new growth is bursting forth from below showing that the tree is still ready to take on a few more years yet.

Approaching the last Sister across the garden I was confronted by an aged being, seemingly struggling up to meet me, its two huge lateral boughs propped like a pensioner with two sticks. I almost expected the tree-beast beyond to shuffle forward through the bluebells beneath its rugged old frame.

The Peace Tree

57 Map D2

When Wales abounds with yews and oaks of great age or significance it comes as something of a surprise to discover a relatively modest sycamore tree in the town square of Caerwys, in Flintshire, which represents the essence of a national custom more than 800 years old.

The vibrant tradition of eisteddfodau in Wales – festivals of literature, music and performance – is still flourishing in the twenty-first century, with both the international gathering each year at Llangollen and the annual national event which moves around the country. The earliest eisteddfod can be traced back to 1176 at Cardigan Castle, but a strong vein of musical, literary and poetic talent has traditionally brought like-minded folk together, whether formally or informally, all over Wales on a regular basis for hundreds of years. As with many traditions, they have waxed and waned in popularity over time.

Caerwys holds the unusual accolade of being the smallest town in Great Britain to have been granted a Royal Charter; an honour bestowed by King Edward I in 1290. An eisteddfod of some description is known to have occurred in the town long before the sixteenth century, but it took an edict from Queen Elizabeth I in 1568 to formalize matters (perhaps the Royal Charter status focused the monarch's attention on the town), making Caerwys 'the home of the Eisteddfod'. Henceforth all participants were able to gather around the tree in the square, composing, perfecting and performing their pieces before entering the town hall to be judged. Success effectively gave those who achieved it a early form of celebrity status, a recognition of their remarkable gift or talent that set them above the common street entertainers or buskers and gave them the right to offer their services as qualified performing artists.

The custom of the eisteddfod had all but disappeared by the turn of the eighteenth century in Caerwys, but it was revived in 1819. Some wonderful Victorian photographs, taken about 1875, of the old sycamore growing from its stone plinth show a motley assemblage of local folk gathered about the old tree. The tree appears to be in excess of 100 years old at this time, but also it is situated right in the very middle of the crossroads. It's clear from these images that the old tree had recently been trimmed back, but the overall condition of the structure looks poor.

Wet collodion plates c1875 thought to be by John Thomas, show the Peace Tree at the centre of the crossroads in Caerwys – viewed southwards. Clearly this was a big day for the village and many of the locals have turned out to be recorded for posterity along with the tree.

Above: The Peace Tree
– viewed northwards.
The second of John
Thomas's remarkable
early photographs.

It must be assumed that this tree didn't make it far into the twentieth century,
since in 1919 a replacement sycamore was planted. This time the stone plinth
was relocated in the north-east corner of the town square, presumably
removing a potential road hazard for those newfangled motor cars. At this
point, in thankful commemoration of the end of the Great War, the new planting
was named the Peace Tree.

Latterly the 1919 tree finally succumbed to the rigours of old age and had to
be felled when it became dangerous; so in March 1968 the Earl of Plymouth
planted the present incarnation of this famous sycamore, which looks to be
set fair for a good while longer.

Gresford Yew

58 Map D2

Above: Engraving of the Gresford Yew from Arboretum et Fruticetum Britannicum 1838.

The village of Gresford, a little to the north-east of Wrexham, boasts a churchyard full of fine yew trees that have arguably been the best documented of all Welsh yews during the last 200 years. Almost every authority writing about Welsh trees chose to mention Gresford and, in particular, its mightiest denizen, with a current girth of 29 feet 7 inches (9.0 metres) at 4 feet above ground, hunched in sombre splendour in the south-east corner of the churchyard. It would appear, somewhat bizarrely, that this male tree has long been known as 'the Old Lady'.

Some of the following records and quotes have been methodically assembled by several yew enthusiasts, including Allen Meredith, Reg Wheeler and Tim Hills of the Ancient Yew Group.

The earliest record stems from the quaintly named, *The Orthodox Churchman's Magazine; or a Treasury of Divine and Useful knowledge* of 1801, with a simple and brief mention of, '...the great yew tree now growing in the churchyard at Gresford, in North Wales, which is nine yards and nine inches [in girth]'.

In the 1813 publication *Rural Sports*, William Barker Daniel provides the first comprehensive description of both the great old tree and other younger yews in the churchyard.

'...hunched in sombre splendour in the south-east corner of the churchyard.'

'In the churchyard at Gresford ... are growing nineteen Yew Trees. The dimensions of one of them was taken in May 1808, and it is mentioned as a most singular Vegetable Production – the circumference of the Body [bole] of this said Yew Tree, one foot from the ground, is the enormous size of seven yards eighteen inches; at five feet from the ground, is nine yards nine inches; two of the great arms are dead, and two more are following rapidly, yet there still remains a sound Body, and seven large Arms that are still in a thriving state; and probably will survive another Hundred Years, before it will drop amongst the Graves of the Dead, which it has so many Centuries shaded. This tree has stood in the reign of seventeen Kings and three Queens ...'

By 1833 J.E. Bowman was moved to write in the *Magazine of Natural History* on the longevity of yew trees, extrapolating an approximate age for the Gresford Yew of 1,419 years by using the known planting dates and average sizes of the other 18 yews planted in 1726.

'...the Gresford Yew is most probably somewhere between 1500 and 2000 years old...'

Two slightly confusing references to the younger yews were brought to light in G.S. Jarman's *The Village of Gresford* in 1912, where he cites an item in the churchwardens accounts for 1710 – 'paid to John Powell, for watering and hedging about the young yew trees, 2s.' He also mentions another entry in the registers of births – 'mem.: that in the year 1726 there were 25 young yew trees planted in the Churchyard'. Were the trees referred to in 1710 perhaps the nursery bed for the same trees that were actually planted out in 1726? No matter, for it would appear that seven of these young trees must have died by the time the account of 1813 was written. As recently as 1984 Reg Wheeler visited the churchyard and recorded 33 younger yews, but there is no way of knowing which were the 1726 trees, so age extrapolations today are well nigh impossible.

Perhaps suffice to say that the Gresford Yew is most probably somewhere between 1,500 and 2,000 years old, which would pitch it conveniently into an age range where a traditional yet unfounded association might apply. It is said that the tree was planted around AD 350 by the widow of a Roman officer stationed at nearby Chester; a carved stone placed over the grave and the yew planted as a symbol of immortality.

Unfortunately the tree appears, from the partially blackened interior, to have suffered damage from fire long ago, which is perhaps why the iron railings were erected – a sad indictment of our forebears. Surely we now live in more enlightened times where we value and protect such venerable trees? After all, hundreds of other ancient yews survive across Britain without this intrusive protection. So might it not be a good idea to release this great old yew from its prison so that all those visitors who cherish such magnificent trees can get closer to the spirit of its antiquity and mystery and, yes, perhaps even hug it!

Overton-on-Dee Yews

59 Map E2

Above: Church of
St. Mary the Virgin,
Overton-on-Dee,
with its 'circle' of
yews c1820.

O verton is a pleasant village to the south of Wrexham that has become renowned for the unusual feature of a ring of yew trees that encircle the church of St. Mary the Virgin set back from the broad High Street. Yew circles, seldom as complete as this one, feature around a handful of Welsh churches and are popularly supposed to indicate a pre-Christian sacred site. Without doubt this is a delightful churchyard with its 23 dark, sentinel yews marking out the boundary and yet, after much contemplation, one has to question whether this really is a circle.

This yew formation first receives mention in an obscure publication of 1802, and around the same time it would appear that a visiting English tourist was moved to write a few lyrical lines about his tour of north Wales. Entitled 'The Seven Wonders of Wales' the anonymously written rhyme was obviously much reported and repeated and runs thus:

> Pistyll Rhaeadr and Wrexham Steeple
> Snowdon's mountain without its people
> Overton yew trees, St. Winefride Wells
> Llangollen Bridge, and Gresford Bells.

Given the nature of this list one has to wonder how widely this tourist roamed to come up with such a shortlist, as there are many more 'wonders' that could topple these, particularly in the realms of the churchyard yew, but once in print the reputations of these sites grew out of all proportion, and it would seem that this acclamation for Overton soon increased its significance as an unmissable attraction for tourists. Engavings of the church with its yews were published, and by the turn of the nineteenth century all the major postcard publishers had Overton High Street with its great yews billowing over the church wall as part of their range. Vaughan Cornish in his *The Churchyard Yew and Immortality* (1946) mentions that, 'The colossal Yews form one of the "Seven Wonders of Wales".' One suspects that he never actually saw them in order to put them in context with the numerous other much larger trees that he wrote about.

Without wishing to diminish the fame of these trees my own personal observations walking around the churchyard are of a more rectilinear site rather than circular. The oldest yew, recently fenced in for its own protection, is 15 feet 8 inches (4.8 metres) in girth, in all probability taking its age back about 600–700 years and neatly coinciding with the thirteenth-century founding of the church. The rest of the yews must have been planted subsequently.

In 1992 the village celebrated a 700 year anniversary since it was granted a Royal Charter by Edward I in 1292. To mark the event the Queen visited and planted another yew tree.

Llangollen Whitebeam

Right: A stunning rock whitebeam on the cliff top.

To the north of Llangollen lies the Eglwyseg Valley, overlooked by the mighty, tiered limestone crags and underlying screes which stretch for four and a half miles along the northern side. Numerous small trees may be seen issuing from improbably tiny cracks and hollows in the sheer cliff-face. The darker patches of green indicate yew trees which, although small and convoluted in form, may easily be many centuries old. Ash, rowan and hawthorn are also much in evidence, but the specialities here are the whitebeams. These are divided into two species – rock whitebeam (*Sorbus rupicola*), a tree with a wide national distribution, and the site-specific Llangollen whitebeam (*Sorbus cuneifolia*). Of this latter tree, there are about 240 specimens growing along a two mile stretch of the crags. This is the only place in Britain that this tree grows.

'...trees may be seen issuing from improbably tiny cracks and hollows in the sheer cliff-face.'

Quite remarkably there is a very early illustration of this whitebeam growing on nearby Castell Dinas Bran in the third edition of W. Hudson's *Flora Anglica* in 1798, although its extremely localised, endemic status was not appreciated at the time. Botanists A.J. Wilmott and E.F. Warburg both realised it was something distinctive, but declined to actually record it as a separate named species. Indeed, until a few years ago Llangollen whitebeam was classified as a slight variation of *Sorbus anglica*, and only in recent years did it receive the appellation *Sorbus cuneifolia*, a name derived from the narrower cuneate base to the leaves.

While most of the locally defined habitats of recently named, rare Welsh whitebeams are confined to south-east Wales this is one of only three species that grows in north Wales. Stirton's whitebeam (*Sorbus stirtoniana*) was described and named by Rich and Proctor in 2009 in honour of Professor Charles Stirton for his work establishing the National Botanic Garden of Wales. About 40 specimens grow only on the north and west crags of Craig Breidden in Montgomeryshire (much of which is in the confines of a private quarry).

Pages 204–205: Evening sunlight on
Craigiau Eglwyseg.
Above / right: Llangollen whitebeam
clings to the edge of the limestone crags
on Craigiau Eglwyseg. The cropped stems
below show just how far the sheep are
prepared to reach for these tasty leaves.

The third tree, being a hitherto unnamed taxon commonly known at present as Menai Strait whitebeam, numbers about 30 specimens growing above the shoreline at Nantporth. Even though it was first observed in the late nineteenth century, it is fascinating to think that more than a century on it is still the source of conjecture regarding its origins; research is currently ongoing into its status and classification.

Because so much of the interpretation of all these rare whitebeams has been disseminated over the last 20 years, largely as a result of the new technology available to unravel their genetic make-up, it casts the intriguing prospect of how many more whitebeams are out there waiting to be identified.

Pontfadog Oak

Tucked quietly away behind a hillside farmhouse above the village of Pontfadog in the Ceiriog Valley stands what is arguably Wales' oldest and largest oak. A sessile oak (*Quercus petraea*), this great old stager, still clinging precariously to life is considered by some to be about 1,200 years old. It must have already been a substantial tree in 1165, when tradition asserts that a Welsh army, raised by Owain Gwynedd and an alliance of Welsh princes in response to Henry II's invading army, gathered beneath this tree before the battle of Crogen, a short distance down the valley to the east. There is no way of verifying this claim, but it serves as a historically romantic and patriotic rallying point to this day.

In 1850 the owner of the tree at that time discovered two gold chisels that had been hidden in the trunk. They were apparently on view locally in 1880 but their subsequent fate is unknown. Given that gold is such a soft metal, it seems rather strange that chisels should be made of it, but perhaps these served some symbolic importance. During the nineteenth century many ancient and historic trees were recorded by artists, travellers and historians, but the Pontfadog Oak appears to have been completely overlooked until the turn of the century, when the explosion of the craze for sending postcards finally throws up a delightful image of a little lad standing beneath the great tree (see p.24). Judging by this Edwardian image it would seem that the tree's trunk has today reduced quite considerably in volume over about six foot above ground. Whether this was down to pollarding or boughs simply falling off or rotting away is unknown.

'...arguably Wales' oldest and largest oak.'

The present owner recalls that, as a teenager in 1963, she heard a loud noise and thought that the chimney had fallen over, only to find that a large limb had fallen off the tree on to the farmhouse. The tree began to deteriorate, so a little later the International Hermeneutic Society from nearby Llangollen, whose members frequently visited the oak, sponsored the fitting of a steel support band to hold the crown together. During the last few years the ancient oak has been falling further into decline, with some large and ominous cracks appearing in the old bole. Clearly the safety of those living beneath the tree is paramount, so new methods of remedial work are currently under discussion. It would be very sad to lose such a special tree, although it has probably grown about as old as any oak can. When ancient yews seem virtually immortal,

Photo by Burns

argest Oak Tree in the United Kingdom, Pontfadog (Ceiriog Valley). (17 yds. in circumference)

Above: An Edwardian postcard of the mighty Pontfadog Oak confirms its status as the largest oak tree in the United Kingdom with a girth of 17 yards.

nobody knows for sure why ancient oaks seem to finally give up the struggle at around 1200–1300 years of age.

The Edwardian postcards claimed it to be 'the largest oak in the United Kingdom, 17 yards around', a measurement almost certainly taken at ground level. Today, the tree can still lay claim to that record, but now based on its girth measurement of 42 feet 5 inches (12.9 metres), at 5 feet above ground.

Whatever may befall the Pontfadog Oak in the future, its genetic legacy is assured, for in 1999 two saplings grown by Tanya Austin of Llangennech were presented to the National Botanic Garden of Wales. The image of the tree has also been adopted as a logo for Pontfadog primary school.

Great Oak at the Gates of the Dead

B efore ever clapping eyes on this tree its name has already stirred up some vivid images. Could it be a tree with ancient Celtic mythological associations, or perhaps a hanging tree, or even a place where some dastardly deed was committed?

62 Map D2

Until 2007 few, if any, people knew about this great oak tree, tucked peacefully down in a slight depression of scrub vegetation, beside the road through the Ceiriog Valley, a couple of miles west of Chirk. Rob McBride (aka 'the Tree Hunter') interviewed a local lady about the tree. It transpired that the location had been the scene of a fearsome and bloody battle back in the twelfth century.

In 1165 King Henry II, with bold plans to conquer Wales, raised an army at Oswestry and marched to confront an alliance of Welsh princes, led by Owain Gwynedd. Hearing of this the Welsh army rushed to confront them at the border. When Henry reached the Ceiriog Valley his army suffered repeated ambushes by the Welsh, who had taken cover among the dense woodland above the valley. The king ordered 2,000 woodsmen to fell the trees, so that his army might pass through the valley in safety. Legend has it that this one oak tree was spared. In 1165 it was probably little more than a sapling, so probably of no account anyway. Even though the woodsmen were protected by a powerful vanguard of pikemen the Welsh chose to engage with the English at a point in the valley near the alignment of Offa's Dyke, latterly known as Adwy'r Beddau or 'the Pass of the Graves', in what has come to be known as the Battle of Crogen, the Welsh proving the victors with the English army sustaining heavy losses. Their ranks destroyed, the English ploughed on to the Berwyn Mountains, but soon after, cut off from supplies and battered by foul weather, they were obliged to withdraw from Wales.

Tradition has it that the field on the opposite side of the road to the great oak tree was where the many English dead were buried – an area known as 'the Gates of the Dead'. To this day the field has never been ploughed, but some archaeological survey work to prove or disprove the story would be fascinating.

Rob, with his usual zeal, realised that this was a powerful association and a great excuse to ordain the huge oak tree, some 34 feet (10.4 metres) in girth, with its new and mysterious sounding name – 'The Great Oak at the Gates of the Dead'. Very soon, the tree was getting much publicity – its new name almost certainly arousing considerable interest, and Rob was back there filming with the BBC *Countryfile* programme in 2009. All this attention vindicates the naming of the tree; for with a name, a history, and a rattling good yarn, ancient trees get noticed and nurtured – it's an ideal way of helping to conserve them for the future.

However, after many centuries the old tree finally collapsed in the harsh winter weather of February 2010. Being an old pollard, untended for probably well over a century, the tree had rotted in the middle and split in two, the lesser half still partially attached in spite of falling away and lying on the ground. Many years of water running down into the hollowing centre of the tree as well as an accumulation of much soggy detritus would have caused the rotting process, but it was believed that the extremely low temperatures had then caused icing inside the tree which had expanded and caused the split. It seems like a sad end for the great tree, but it will almost certainly carry on living, even in its semi-recumbent state for a long time to come.

Tan-y-Pistyll
Wild Cherries

63 Map D3

Trees grow around field boundaries wherever you may travel. Some are trimmed or laid into tight and well-managed, stock-proof hedges, while others are left to grow into mature trees; sometimes as maidens, sometimes as pollards. Oak, ash and beech are common large broadleaf species, often bolstered by hawthorn, holly, field maple or hazel, but to find wild cherry as a field boundary tree, and huge specimens to boot, is something very much out of the ordinary.

Most visitors are drawn along the tortuous single-track road that leads up the Rhaeadr Valley from Llanrhaeadr-ym-Mochnant by the lure of the superb waterfall at Pistyll Rhaeadr (the little café at the bottom of the falls is quite tasty too). However, just before the falls and the rather abrupt end to the valley road which the falls oblige, a field on the south side of the road contains four absolutely enormous wild cherry trees which can be confidently described as the largest of their species in the whole of Wales.

These trees are incredibly knobbly, with burry and buttressed boles that make them extremely difficult to measure, but their girths range from 12 feet 4 inches (3.76 metres) to 14 feet 2 inches (4.32 metres). When first encountered in full flower in April they appeared as something of a surprise, and it was instantly apparent from the absence of other cherry blossom beacons that this was not a common tree in the valley. Someone, at some time, must surely have planted these for a reason, almost certainly not for the cherries which are small and extremely sour, but more likely for the timber – a beautiful wood for cabinet makers as well as wood turnery. Wild cherries are not usually expected to last much more than 100 years at best, but the suspicion here is that these trees could be in excess of 200 years old.

Their visual statement in the landscape makes one wonder why more use is not made of wild cherry. The great pale pink clouds of springtime flowering as well as the rich golden glow of autumn foliage which, in the best years for colour, attain a startling vermilion, make this tree indispensable.

'Their visual statement in the landscape makes one wonder why more use is not made of wild cherry.'

Pennant Melangell Yews

64 Map D3

In a remote valley tucked beneath the Berwyn Mountains lies the tiny settlement of Pennant Melangell. A narrow lane from the village of Llangynog leads you into this secret and special place; a tranquil retreat, a place of contemplation and undoubtedly of deep spiritual significance for thousands of years.

The church of St. Melangell stands squat and square-towered, as it has for the last 1,200 years, amid the Christian memorials and pre-Christian yew tree sentinels of this sacred site. The four great yews, two male and two female trees, are believed to be around 2,000 years old, and stand on the perimeter of a circular enclosure, asserting the site's Bronze Age credentials. Although the trees are hollow, and some have lost major limbs in the distant past, they are all still in remarkably good health.

'A narrow lane from the village of Llangynog leads you into this secret and special place…'

The story of St. Melangell has been handed down in Welsh folklore for hundreds of years, and is recorded in a seventeenth-century manuscript. Like all traditional tales there are variations and embellishments to the story, but it is said that Melangell arrived in the valley from Ireland, reputedly a princess rejecting her courtly and privileged existence or perhaps fleeing a forced marriage, in order to lead a life of prayer and devotion. Legend relates how one Brochwel Yscythrog, Prince of Powys, was out hunting when his hounds

Above: Medieval oak rood screen in the church at Pennant Melangell depicting the story of St. Melangell.

gave chase to a hare. The frightened creature entered a thicket where the maiden Melangell was at prayer, taking refuge beneath the folds of her cloak. When the prince urged his hounds on to retrieve the hare, instead they fled howling. The prince was so impressed by her courage and sanctity that he gave her the valley where she was able to establish a religious community for women. To this day hares are known in this locality as 'Melangell's lambs', and have never been hunted.

The church contains the twelfth-century shrine of Melangell, to which many still make a pilgrimage to honour the saint and seek healing. The Romanesque shrine, said to be one of the finest in Britain, was dismantled at the Reformation, but the stones were used in other parts of the church so that in 1958 it was possible to retrieve these stones and restore and rebuild it in the chancel where it had originally stood. St. Melangell is still known as the patron saint of hares and there is a beautiful fifteenth-century oak rood screen in the church which depicts the story of Melangell and Prince Brochwel.

On the day I first visited Pennant Melangell I recall a silent prayer to the sun not to set before I reached the church, for it was late in the day and I feared that the valley would soon been sunk in deep shadow. As I walked in through the handsome stone lychgate the whole churchyard was bathed in that glorious, low, evening light that enhances and saturates all the colours. The boles of the ancient yews glowed orange gold, and I began to catch this light while I still had time. Even as I worked against the dipping day I looked to the west and was astounded to see the line of the sun marking perfect time along the crest of the dark silhouette of the hills, and it struck me that whoever first marked out this place as somewhere sacred didn't choose it at random. They knew exactly what they were doing.

The Patriarch Tree

65 Map D3

Above: Sketch of the yew in Llanerfyl churchyard as published by the Anastatic Drawing Society in 1863.

The tiny village of Llanerfyl, which bestrides the A458 from Welshpool to Dolgellau, is most ordinarily whizzed past by each and every motorist with a journey to complete and no knowledge whatsoever of the remarkable treat that squats in convoluted antiquity within St. Erfyl's churchyard.

Known as the Patriarch Tree this yew consists of four tumbled, twisted and partially supported boles – three female and one male – that have spread themselves out from one central, shallow mound to cover a very large part of the churchyard. Generally speaking yew trees are dioecious (separate male and female trees), but it is known that yews can, on rare occasions, have both male and female elements in one tree – monoecious. Some observers of this particular yew believe that it is actually two different trees fused together near the base, but only a DNA sampling will solve the conundrum for certain.

Although the current church building only dates back to 1870, there has been a church on the site since the late-sixth or early-seventh century, and clearly, prior to this period the site had some sacred significance; a curvilinear churchyard suggesting pre-Christian roots. Also, a fifth-or sixth-century Roman English stone was unearthed from beneath the yew in 1915, indicating a site associated with burials. There is every chance that this yew with its girth of some 35 feet (10.7 metres) at the base has been here for around 2,000 years, so it is perfectly feasible that it was a powerful symbol of rebirth and of the

eternity of the soul to the Romans who buried their kinsmen here. The founding of the church by St. Erfyl also ties in with a nearby well, which was 400 metres north-west of the church; again indicating the possible site of an early saint cell.

The tree receives its first written recognition in Lewis's *Topographical Dictionary of Wales* in 1849, but comes to greater prominence in 1863 when, most unusually, a sketch is made of the tree and published by the Anastatic Drawing Society. Early renditions of Welsh yews are few and far between, but this delightful drawing faithfully reflects the distinctive nature of the tree, as well as revealing that over the last 150 years it has collapsed and spread to a greater degree. All ancient yews are unique, but this one is arguably a little more unique than most.

Buttington Oak

'...one of the most impressive oak trees in the whole of Wales.'

66 Map D3

A short walk north from the village of Buttington, along the eastern banks of the River Severn, brings you to one of the most impressive oak trees in the whole of Wales. There are many oaks dotted around the fields hereabouts, but this behemoth outstrips them all.

Whilst having some sort of unusual history or special association does add an extra dimension to a heritage tree, sometimes they simply announce themselves by their remarkable size. The Buttington Oak is one such tree.

Despite searching through various archives and publications, and even resorting to local hearsay and traditions, absolutely nothing has tied this tree to a fascinating story. So, suffice to say, it is a huge English oak tree (*Quercus robur*), and at 36 feet 2 inches (11.03 metres) the third largest in the whole of Wales. It grows fairly close to the projected line of Offa's Dyke and may once have performed a role as a boundary tree although, quite clearly, even with a guesstimated age of around 800–900 years it wasn't around in the eighth century when King Offa ordered the construction of the dyke. There are no obvious physical remains of Offa's Dyke at this particular location, and boundaries may have moved to and fro over the centuries, but the present day boundary is only a couple of miles to the east and in the past the River Severn has performed boundary duties, so it would seem highly feasible that the oak was a significant landmark.

It was only as recently as 2009 that the tree was recognised for its extreme size and antiquity by Veronica Henry, who logged her discovery with the Ancient Tree Hunt. A critical examination of the tree reveals it to be in the best of health, although some might say the severe trampling around the base by livestock could lead to deleterious consequences due to compaction. It is possible, but to be perfectly frank the tree has survived many centuries, almost certainly serving as shade and protection for livestock during much of that time, with no visible signs of distress. It looks set for a few centuries more.

Buttington Yew

To the north of Welshpool and east of the gentle meanders of the attendant River Severn lies the little village of Buttington. A conundrum that has long surrounded this settlement has been whether or not there was a bloody battle here in the late ninth century, between marauding Vikings and a combined English and Welsh army.

The *Anglo-Saxon Chronicle* of AD 894 certainly documents a Battle of Buttington, where the English under Alfred the Great along with the Welsh under King Merfyn of Powys besieged an army of Vikings under Prince Haesten (some other sources cite the date as 893), but fails to pinpoint the exact location, since another village of Buttington lies on the Severn estuary in Gloucestershire. There are proponents for both locations, for as yet the archaeological evidence for either site is slender. The tradition that it was the Powys site probably stems from a seemingly macabre early nineteenth century discovery. In 1838, while laying the foundations of the new village school on the south-west corner of the churchyard, a burial pit was uncovered which contained 400 skulls and an assortment of limbs which, it is said, bore scars inflicted by battle; hence the assumption that these must have been victims of the carnage.

The nineteenth-century accounts are vivid and reveal the ferocity of the engagement. Edward Mogg in his 1829 edition of *Paterson's Roads* describes the event thus:

'Buttington, the Butdigingtune of the Saxons, is remarkable as having been the scene of a most sanguinary contest between the Danes and the Saxons in the year 894; the former, after traversing the kingdom from east to west, finding themselves pursued by the generals of Alfred, took a course towards Wales, and made a desperate stand at this place, but being very closely blockaded, they were absolutely obliged to eat their horses for want of other subsistence, after which, being reduced by famine and despair to the utmost extremity, they attempted to force their way through the Saxons, who cut them to pieces with the greatest slaughter, leaving very few to relate the disaster.'

'...there was a bloody battle here in the late ninth century...'

Above: Misty morning view of the ancient yew in Buttington churchyard.

Some authorities believe that this cache of bones might relate to an eleventh-century battle close by when, in 1039, Gruffydd ap Llewelyn defeated a Mercian army at the Battle of Rhyd-y-Groes (occasionally referred to as the second Battle of Buttington). Other historians have come to the conclusion that these bones are merely an eighteenth-century clear-out of the congested graveyard – a practice that was apparently commonplace up to the nineteenth century. Carbon dating of the skulls might settle these disputes.

Tradition asserts that the largest yew tree in the churchyard, a handsome and healthy male tree, was planted to commemorate the battle around AD 893/4 Its girth of 29 feet 6 inches (9.0 metres) certainly reflects an age of about 1100–1200 years, perhaps even a little older. As with so many of these ancient yews, the tree is hollow. In recent years the bole has developed a dense covering of epicormic shoots which have completely hidden the base of the old tree.

Powis Castle Estate Oaks

'...some of the finest specimen oaks to be found in Wales.'

68 Map D3

Above: Powis Castle, engraved by J.C. Varrall after H. Gastineau, published by Jones & Co. 1831 – steel engraving.
Right: Gwen Morgan's Oak

The extensive deer park surrounding the National Trust property of Powis Castle and Gardens boasts some of the finest specimen oaks to be found in Wales. There has been an enduring tradition on the Powis Castle Estate of growing high quality oak timber, forestry that is still a thriving element of the commercial livelihood of the estate.

Historic accounts of impressive, ancient and individual trees on Welsh estates are few and far between; most documentation tending to dwell on the techniques and schemes of planting, management and harvesting, with much stress on the importance of timber quality and yields. So the visit of H.J. Elwes (co-author of *The Trees of Great Britain and Ireland*) to Powis Castle in 1904 throws a spotlight on some of the park's outstanding oaks. He wrote that, 'In April 1904 the Earl of Powis showed me some trees growing in his ancient park at Powis Castle ... which I believe to be actually the champion oaks of Great Britain at the present time.' A stickler for detail, Elwes records, 'The measurements which I give were made most carefully by Mr. W.F. Addie, agent for the Powis Castle Estates, who used a long ladder and a man to climb nearly all over them and take the length and girth of the principal branches down to

6 inches quarter-girth. I checked the height and girth of the trunks myself as carefully as possible, and believe that the following is a very accurate estimate.'

'The Champion Tree' [latterly 'Oak'] was a maiden hybrid oak, '23 feet 6 inches in girth and a towering 105 feet high.' Although this must clearly have been a tempting target for the forester's axe, given that it was estimated to contain some 2,026 cubic feet of timber, sentiment must have ruled the day and the champion was given a stay of execution. Time and the elements finally took their toll when the great tree fell on 13th April 1939, by which time it was 24 feet (7.3 metres) in girth and 110 feet high – reputedly the largest oak then standing in Britain.

An ancient pollard oak 'Near the Park Plain' had no name, but was the greatest girthed oak in the park by some distance, having a 'girth of 29 feet 7 inches and a height of 95 feet', it being clear from the accompanying photograph taken at that date that it had not been pollarded in many a year. This abandonment of the regime probably led to the tree's eventual demise, even though, at the time of a visit in 2003, there was still a little life left in the old tree, but only just hanging on above the seriously decayed and hollowed bole beneath. In 2009 the old carcass of the tree, known for many years as the Red Rock Oak, finally gave up the ghost, split in two, and died.

Another fine outgrown pollard called 'Lady Powis' Oak' was recorded as '22 feet 6 inches in girth and 95 feet high'. It still exists in a part of the park where, sadly, it cannot be viewed by the public, and now has a girth of 25 feet 5 inches (7.7 metres). A fourth oak was recorded by Elwes in 'Gwen Morgan's Wood' (now known as Keeper's Wood or Peasantries on the old maps). Although we cannot be sure exactly where this tree once stood, this was probably the tree known latterly as Gwen Morgan's Oak.

From left – right, The Red Rock Oak in 2004, when it was still clinging to life; a plate from *Trees of Great Britain and Ireland* – Elwes & Henry, 1904; the dead carcass of the old tree as it stands today.

A huge hybrid oak, mentioned by Linnard, and dubbed 'The Giant' also once flourished in the park, and attained a massive 33 feet 9 inches (10.3 metres) girth and 90 feet (27.4 metres) height by the time it fell in 1961.

Certainly the most impressive and prominent oak that can still be enjoyed by today's visitors sits on a small grassy rise to the right of the exit drive, just beyond the cattle grid, and right in front of what was formerly known as Gwen Morgan's Wood. There is a strong likelihood that this tree is in fact Gwen Morgan's Oak. It is an extremely fine specimen of sessile oak (*Quercus petraea*), grasping the earth with mighty buttressing roots and, although a little stag-headed in parts of the canopy, still in very good health. The girth measures 25 feet 8 inches (7.8 metres) and the tree is 66 feet (20.12 metres) high.

The Powis Castle Estate is very proud of its splendid trees and hopes that all who drive through the parkland to visit the castle derive much pleasure from seeing them. However, they do wish to stress that the park is private and not open for the public to roam at will.

![Photograph of Powis Castle viewed through honeysuckle foliage, with a laburnum arch and formal gardens in the foreground]

Yews of Powis Castle

69 Map D3

An early spring morning in the gardens of Powis Castle can be magical; watching the first weak sunlight creeping out above Leighton, burning through the recalcitrant Severn Valley mists, picking its way between mighty oaks on wilderness ridge, imparting an even ruddier glow to the towering red sandstone ramparts of the medieval castle on its rocky mound.

Unlike so many of the castles of the Marches, which were built by the English to keep the Welsh in check, Powis was actually owned by a dynasty of Welsh princes until the latter part of the thirteenth century. In 1587 the estate was sold to the Herbert family, and from then on the gardens went through many

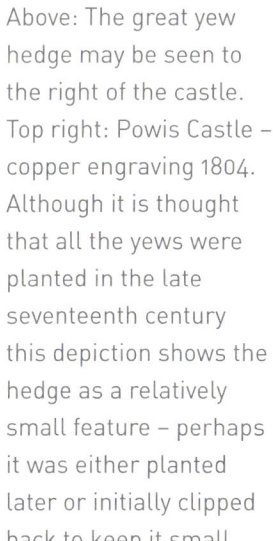

Above: The great yew hedge may be seen to the right of the castle. Top right: Powis Castle – copper engraving 1804. Although it is thought that all the yews were planted in the late seventeenth century this depiction shows the hedge as a relatively small feature – perhaps it was either planted later or initially clipped back to keep it small.

phases of development and change, but the yew tree topiary in particular was nurtured along the top of the 600 foot long terraces below the south-east façade. The terraces were probably the work of architect William Winde, around 1660, and the yews were planted shortly afterwards in about 1680. Garden design tended to follow fashionable trends and, in the late seventeenth century, topiary, a popular feature of both French and Dutch gardens, came to the fore in the Britain of William and Mary.

The yews along the top terrace at Powis are thought to have once been cut into cones and pyramids and, undoubtedly, the monstrous yew hedge which tumbles down the northern end of the terraces must surely have had considerably more formality to its form. The eighteenth century, with its great faux-naturalistic landscape architects such as Kent, Brown and Repton, produced something of a backlash against the tight formality of garden design epitomised by topiary, resulting in such lavishly manicured gardens being obliterated or, at best, the trees were simply permitted to grow back into their natural shapes.

In 1780 Gilpin bemoaned the practice of topiary: 'The yew is, of all other trees, the most tonsile. Hence all the indignities it suffers. We everywhere see it cut and metamorphosed into such a variety of deformities, that we are hardly brought to conceive it has a natural shape.' By 1838 J.C. Loudon observed that

'...dark green blobs of the yews emanate from beneath the castle like some oversize colony of giant fungi.'

very little topiary had survived in British gardens and was beginning to wonder whether a revival might be in order – 'The effect of these [topiarised yews] is so striking and singular, that we are surprised the taste has not, to a certain extent been revived. This, we have no doubt, it will be, in the gardens to Gothic and Elizabethan villas, as soon as men exercise their reason in matters of this kind, and do not allow themselves to be led indiscriminately by fashion.' Accordingly, from about this time, something of a topiary renaissance began, later to be championed by followers of the Arts and Crafts Movement, so that the shaggy, unkempt yews reappeared once more in their neat, clipped and often fanciful manifestations. In decrying the caprices of garden fashion the influential Loudon had sewn the seeds of another one.

Left: The yew topiary
along the upper terrace
at Powis Castle.
Below: The author with
the hedge towering
far above.
Below right: The inside
of one of the topiarised
yews.

At Powis, one suspects that the gardeners of the nineteenth century had the desire to clip, but had clearly lost the vision of the original seventeenth century topiary. In 1952 the castle and gardens were bequeathed to the National Trust by the Herbert family and ever since a gently evolving programme of enhancing the gardens has continued. Today the billowing, dark green blobs of the yews emanate from beneath the castle like some oversize colony of giant fungi. The hedge, towering 50 feet (15.24 metres) high, and surely the highest yew hedge in Britain, is a magnificent cascade of lost forms which looks as if you could run and jump down it like some sort of giant bouncy castle. Of course you can't. Only in the last few years have the gardeners been able to access the hedge for its annual 'haircut' with a cherry-picker machine; prior to that it was a very precarious job undertaken from massive ladders. It is fascinating to walk beneath this huge hedge, to enjoy the gnarled and contorted forms of the old yew boles and roots – the very scaffolding that has held the hedge aloft these last 300 years.

Charles Ackers'
Redwood Grove

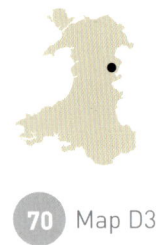

F or more than 40 years now a growing band of long-distance route trekkers have threaded their way along the Offa's Dyke Path as it breasts the gentle slopes of Moel y Mab, just a few miles south-east of Welshpool. Although dense forestry shrouds most of the hill there are still occasional glimpses of impressive sweeping views down into the Severn Valley spread far below. However, few could suspect that no more than a stone's throw below them lies a perfect little slice of California.

Leighton Hall, a grand mid-nineteenth century residence was built between 1850 and 1856 for John Naylor, who had received the estate as a wedding present from his uncle, Christopher Leyland (a name for tree buffs to conjure with). The house and its accompanying farms and parkland still constitute a fine estate to this day, but all is private, so not open to the public. John Naylor was bitten by the Victorian craze to plant exotic trees – with the usual vogue plantings of monkey puzzles and Wellingtonias, as well as an eclectic mix of pines, firs, spruces, hemlocks and cedars from around the world – in his pinetum, presently known as the Naylor Pinetum. Hard by the pinetum, on the western slopes of Moel y Mab, is the Charles Ackers' Redwood Grove which today is arguably the largest grove of coast redwoods (*Sequoia sempervirens*) in the whole of Europe.

Fossil records reveal that millions of years ago the redwoods had a vast global range. Today, the last surviving native colony is to be found in a 35–40 mile wide coastal band stretching almost 500 miles through California and into southern Oregon where the tree thrives in dense groves, regularly shrouded in sea fog, creating the moisture-laden atmosphere that the species craves. Due to the phenomenal demand for redwood timber, particularly during the nineteenth century, some 96 per cent of these trees have been felled in the last 150 years – a frightening statistic but one that has now been halted by energetic bands of conservationists. Although the tree was first discovered in 1769 the first introductions to Britain were not until 1843. In 1857 John Naylor brought 33 seedlings back from California. They seemed to do rather well on the sheltered slopes above Leighton, so more were planted on a regular basis until today the grove covers about 12 hectares.

'...the largest grove of coast redwoods in the whole of Europe.'

Above: In the foreground a cut stump may be seen regenerating – a common occurrence among broadleaf species but rare among conifers.

One particular tree (planted in 1863), has proved a remarkable symbol of the species' ability to naturally regenerate in the wake of disaster. In 1936 a ferocious storm hit the grove and several trees were laid low. As foresters will, they chopped up and carted away most of the debris, but for some unknown reason one tree was left where it had fallen. Maybe it had been noted that the root system was not entirely severed, and curiosity let it lie. Clearly the remaining roots gave initial succour, but where the shattered boughs underneath had dug deep into the forest floor upon impact new root systems began to develop. The boughs on the top of the prostrate tree began to head upwards seeking the light – a dozen or more of them. Today about half of these have matured into substantial trees growing in a neat line along the old trunk.

A fallen coast redwood has taken root
along its length and now supports six
substantial trees.

'It has the capacity to throw up suckers from its shallow root system, or can produce burls (woody lignotubers), either on the roots or aerial ones which drop to earth...'

This is almost certainly a unique occurrence in Britain but is typical of forest regeneration in North American forests. Coast redwood is a born survivor, being one of the few conifers which, like the majority of broadleaf trees, can be coppiced; witness the numerous burgeoning stumps dotted around the grove. It has the capacity to throw up suckers from its shallow root system, or can produce burls (woody lignotubers), either on the roots or aerial ones which drop to earth and, like giant primeval tree 'eggs', upon hitting the ground can push out roots and shoots, giving birth to yet another young redwood.

The biggest coast redwood in the States and indeed the world's tallest tree is one named 'Hyperion', an impressive 379 feet (115.5 metres) high. The oldest trees are in excess of 2,000 years old. Leighton's redwood grove seems a mere nursery by comparison, with the tallest trees around 130 feet (40 metres) high. They have a little way to go yet.

The Charles Ackers' Redwood Grove was gifted to the Royal Forestry Society at a special ceremony in the woods in 1958 by Sir Charles, who was then owner of the Leighton Estate. This is a private wood, and permission to visit must be sought from the Royal Forestry Society.

Garthmyl Oak

71 Map D3

own the centuries a handful of historically significant and ancient oaks in Wales have received due recognition by some special appellation – currently the most famous is the huge Pontfadog Oak (see p.208), while historically it might be the rugged old Nannau Oak with its gruesome tale to tell (see p.30). Burrowing through the archives of the National Library of Wales a pair of fascinating images came to light of the Garthmyl Oak – two photographs from around 1860; one taken in winter, one in summer, of this massive, named oak tree. Clearly it was of great note and interest 150 years ago, but for anything beyond its great age and size is unclear.

About a mile south of Berriew, in the Severn Valley, lies the hamlet of Garthmyl. The old photographs were a good guide to identifying the tree, but finding it might have proven tricky. Large, old pollard trees such as this are often associated with the parkland surrounding historic houses of note. Garthmyl Hall looked like an eminently suitable location to search. Via the lovely people who own the hall today and who, incidentally, have a truly monumental Cedar of Lebanon in their garden (see p.240), I eventually traced the oak I was seeking. It now belongs to the grounds of a nearby house rather than the hall, some of the land having been sold off 25 years ago, but it is still in remarkably good shape considering it is estimated to be 600–800 years old.

Garthmyl Hall, formerly Garthmyl House until the mid-nineteenth century, was in the hands of the Jones family from medieval times up until 1848, when it was sold to a Major-General Gold, who lived there with his wife until 1885. At this date Mrs. Christine Humphreys bought the house, and it would remain in the same family for exactly a century before her great granddaughter, Christine Churchill, finally sold up in 1985.

It was Christine who was kindly able to furnish a little information about the old oak. Her grandfather inherited the estate in 1915, and by the early 1920s there was obviously some concern about the deteriorating state of the tree, to the extent that he was advised to brace and band the branches together with metalwork to prevent potential collapse. This might have seemed like the best way forward in its day, but the latest concern is that this old remedial work now appears to have cut into the branches so deeply that there is a real possibility that they will eventually be severed, rather defeating the original aims of well-intentioned work. Current practice with ancient trees is to avoid metal bracing wherever possible, as it tends to prevent the natural flexing of the tree and can indeed cut into the vascular tissue causing damage.

Christine provides a delightful account of her childhood affection for the old oak:

'As a child growing up I adored this tree and as soon as my legs were long enough I climbed into it, and the westerly-facing branch, which was hollow, became my den and also my refuge when I had obviously misbehaved and needed to escape my mother's annoyance.'

Not only are the great trees with famous associations to be treasured, but surely the sort of memories and relationships with trees, typified by the Garthmyl Oak, are what makes them all personally and individually great within communities large and small, urban and rural throughout the land.

Garthmyl
Cedar of Lebanon

Map D3

Hunting down one heritage tree can sometimes lead to another fortuitous discovery, and so it was with my quest for the Garthmyl Oak. Calling at Garthmyl Hall to enquire about the location of the old oak tree, the owners told me that they no longer owned the land where the oak grows, pointed me in the right direction, but just before I left they informed me that they had a rather fine tree of their own. 'Do pop round the corner and have a look at the cedar,' they encouraged, 'it is rather a good one.'

I walked around the side of the house and was completely bowled over by a strikingly beautiful, huge Cedar of Lebanon (*Cedrus libani*) proudly spreading its luxuriance across the manicured lawns. Set down in something of a recessed garden the tree is in immaculate condition, for here it has been protected from the worst gusts of any gales (wind damage so often causing losses of large branches) and, I am informed, it has an excellent water supply from underground springs.

It transpires that the great tree hunter and recorder Alan Mitchell visited in the early 1980s and was suitably impressed with what he found. Measuring the girth of the tree today arrives at something in excess of 25 feet (7.62 metres) around, but, like so many of these cedars the base of the tree has grown up with a multitude of stems, resembling what Hugh Johnson describes as 'a sort of organ-pipe formation'. Even though the first Cedar of Lebanon was planted at Childrey Rectory in Oxfordshire as far back as 1646, it wasn't until the mid-eighteenth century that they became a highly fashionable and decorative tree to plant. This is almost certainly an eighteenth-century planting.

'Even though the first Cedar of Lebanon was planted at Childrey Rectory in Oxfordshire as far back as 1646, it wasn't until the mid eighteenth century that they became (...) highly fashionable...'

It is always fascinating to muse upon whether or not the landowners who planted these trees, much in the same mode as Victorian planters of monkey puzzles (*Araucaria araucana*) and Wellingtonias (*Sequoiadendron giganteum*), had any real concept of just how huge they would eventually grow. In the case of the Garthmyl tree it fortunately does not block out the light to the house, although it does, along with another smaller cedar, cast a lot of deep shade.

The owners love their tree and tell me that they have had many happy family occasions beneath it. On looking more closely they have even hung a chandelier beneath one of the lower boughs so they can enjoy it by night.

Newtown Black Poplar

73 Map D3

T he native black poplar (*Populus nigra* subsp. *betulifolia*) has something
of a stronghold along the Welsh borders, but becomes quite a rare tree
the further westwards you travel into Wales. So, it is with some surprise
that a huge and handsome specimen has long been a landmark tree in the
centre of Newtown, Powys.

Black poplars are essentially trees that thrive best in floodplain and riverine
habitats, including hedgerows with their attendant ditches, largely because
they need plenty of water. Sadly, throughout the late twentieth century, many
of the most favourable sites for these trees have been drained for agricultural
purposes and hedges have been grubbed out, threatening their survival and
hampering their regeneration. Add to this the fact that black poplars have not
(until very recently) been planted in any number for at least a century, and the
result is that the national population is one that is largely elderly, with trees
frequently in decline.

While there has clearly been quite a lot of development around the old poplar
in Gravel Car Park, it says much for the care taken by the local authorities that
this tree has survived. Its very distinctive arching, leaning bole makes it stand
out from other trees, even other poplars, and poses a readily identifiable
silhouette in winter. As an amenity tree it brings changing colours through the
seasons, with its deep crimson catkins in April, closely followed by vivid green
spring foliage which flutters and rustles in the breeze, and finally it takes on
deep buttery yellows in the autumn.

The Newtown poplar is a male tree, with no known female trees in the whole of Wales – a statistic that rules out the possibilities of pure natural regeneration by sexual reproduction. Poplars, like willows, are very prone to hybridisation, so the possibilities of cross-pollination with introduced black poplar hybrids or clones is the most likely route for reproduction, creating yet more hybrids rather than maintaining the fidelity of the true species. Taking cuttings from the old tree could be productive, but these will only be yet more male trees, and this doesn't extend the gene pool. Planting some young females fairly near the old male tree might help this process along. Such projects are already under way in other parts of Britain, so it is to be hoped that the Welsh trees might be helped in the same way.

Dolfor Sentinel Yews

The great majority of the yews featured in this book are to be found within the protective walls of churchyards throughout Wales, and these very sanctuaries have been the main reason that so many ancient trees have survived for so long. The trees were venerated in pre-Christian times and revered and respected ever since their absorption into the Christian churchyard.

The Laws of Hywel Dda, the Christian king of Wales around 950 (although such laws had probably been in force even earlier than this), state the values of various trees:

> A consecrated Yew, its value is a pound;
> An Oak, its value is six score pence.
> Fifteen pence is the value of a wood Yew-tree.

In various accounts these special trees were referred to as a consecrated yew; a holy yew (*ywen sancti*) or a saint's yew (*taxus sancti*). Hywel Dda enforced a penalty of 60 sheep for removing such a tree. Moreover, it has long been deemed a deed of extremely ill omen to fell a yew. Even today some foresters will not touch the yew, and on some estates it is still a matter for instant dismissal if a woodsmen is found cutting one down.

So this is a strong foundation for the preservation of churchyard yews in particular, but ancient yews are sometimes found in non-ecclesiastical situations. There are yew woods, but mainly in England. There are yews on the remains of ancient settlements, burial mounds, marking wells or springs, in hedgerows where they were particularly useful as boundary markers, and then there are odd individual trees such as the Dolfor Sentinels – out on their own with no obvious affiliations but still obviously planted at some distant date with a purpose in mind.

Driving over the hills from Knighton to Newtown the road begins to dip towards the village of Dolfor and there on the hill above the road stand two very squat veteran yews. The male tree is 14 feet 8 inches (4.47 metres) around, while his companion female tree is 11 feet 4 inches (3.45 metres) so, in theory, their girth should indicate an age of perhaps 400–500 years. However these trees are growing in a very exposed situation and at an elevation of about 850 feet above sea level so there is every likelihood that they

Left: The beautiful interior of one of the Dolfor yews – the texture more like something poured and solidified than grown over many centuries. Like the flames of the fire or the clouds in the sky there are strange beasts hidden within.

could be a lot older. Their purpose is intriguing, for they might have been waymarkers along some ancient track or drovers' road, they might simply have marked a boundary, or maybe they signify a lost sacred site. All one can say is that they are a pair of remarkably handsome little trees, even though they have been battered by storms, nibbled by sheep and stunted and hollowed by time.

We will probably never know their secret, but all these mysteries are part of what makes the yew so fascinating. Let us hope that some of that mystery remains intact forever.

A B C D E

1

IRISH SEA

Liverpool

Llandudno
Prestatyn
Mostyn
Holyhead
Colwyn Bay
Conwy

2

Llangefni
Bodnant Garden
Caerwys
Flint
Bangor
Denbigh
Mold
Chester
Llanddeiniolen
Llangernyw
Pentre-Llanrhaeadr
Caernarfon
Nantglyn
Ruthin

▲
Gresford
SNOWDON
Wrexham
Betws-y-coed
Llangollen
Overton-on-Dee
Porthmadog
Blaenau Ffestiniog
Pontfadog
Chirk

3

Pwllheli
SNOWDONIA
NATIONAL PARK
Bala
Tan-y-Pistyll
Pennant Melangell

Nannau
Barmouth
Dolgellau
Mallwyd
Llanerfyl
Shrewsbury
Welshpool
Buttington
Powis Castle
Tywyn
Machynlleth
Garthmyl
Kingswood

4

Borth
Newtown
Dolfor

Aberystwyth
Llanidloes
ENGLAND
Punt-rhiw-y-groes
Cwmystwyth
Ystrad Meurig
Knighton
Strata Florida Abbey
Llandrindod Wells
Discoed
Llanfihangel-nant-melan
New Quay
Llanafan Fawr
Builth Wells

5

Pentregat
Penrhiw-pâl
Rhandirmwyn
Alltmawr
Cardigan
Lampeter
Hereford
Nevern
Newcastle Emlyn
Hay-on-Wye
Fishguard
Talley Abbey
Llangorse
PEMBROKESHIRE COAST
Defynnog
Brecon
Llanthony
NATIONAL PARK
Aberglasney
Dinefwr Park
BRECON BEACONS
Pencelli
Ross-on-Wye
Ramsey Island
Golden Grove
NATIONAL PARK
Crickhowell
Llanvihangel Crucorney
Carmarthen
Llangattock
Llanelly
Llantilio Crossenny

6

Haverfordwest
Ammanford
Penmoelallt
Abergavenny
THE
Monmouth
BLORENGE
Tregare
Milford Haven
Merthyr Tydfil
Ty Mawr
Bettws Newydd
Cwm
Mamhilad
Llangattock-juxta-Usk
Aberdare
Pontypool
Llanelli
Neath
Llanhennock
Chepstow
Swansea
Caerphilly
Wentwood
St. Pierre Hotel
Bassaleg
Newport
and Country Club
Port Talbot
Cardiff
Bristol
Porthcawl
Bridgend

7

Penarth
BRISTOL CHANNEL
Barry
East Aberthaw

Key
Kilometres
0 10 20 30 40 50 60
0   10   20   30   40
Miles

N

Gazetteer (1–13)

① Golynos Oak

Once grew at Bassaleg, near Newport. Long gone.

(p.26 / map D6)

② Merlin's Oak

In Carmarthen town at the junction of Priory Street and Oak Lane.

Removed in 1978.

(p.28 / map B5)

③ Nannau Oak

Once grew on the Nannau Estate about 3 miles north of Dolgellau, Gwynedd.

Long gone.

(p.30 / map C3)

④ Discoed Yew

In St. Michael's churchyard, Discoed, Powys.

Access: At all times.

On a minor road approx. 3 miles north-west of Presteigne.

(p.34 / map D4)

⑤ Offa's Dyke Oaks

Impressive oak trees to be found at various points along the length of the 177 mile path.

Access: At all times.

(p.36)

⑥ Llanfihangel-nant-Melan Yews

In St. Michael's churchyard, Llanfihangel-nant-Melan, Powys.

Access: At all times.

On the A44, midway between Llandrindod Wells and Kington.

(p.40 / map D4)

⑦ Llanafan Fawr Yew

In St. Afan's churchyard, Llanafan Fawr, Powys.

Access: At all times.

Approx. 5 miles west of Builth Wells on the B4358.

(p.42 / map D4)

⑧ Alltmawr Yew

In St. Mauritius's churchyard, Alltmawr (Abernant), Powys.

Access: At all times.

Approx. 4 miles south of Builth Wells on the A470.

(p.44 / map D5)

⑨ Llanthony Whitebeams

Darren Lwyd crags and Tarren yr Esgob crags, above west side of Ewyas Valley, Powys.

Access: At all times (with care).

(p.46 / map D5)

⑩ Llanvihangel Court Sweet Chestnuts

In pastures to the south of Llanvihangel Court, Llanvihangel Crucorney, Monmouthshire.

Access: At all times (with consideration).

A narrow lane leads from the east side of the A465, opposite the village, up to a group of barns.

The avenue may be seen to one's right.

N.b. This is private land, but the owners are happy for visitors to view the trees.

Please park vehicles responsibly, shut all gates behind you and keep dogs on leads.

(p.50 / map D5)

⑪ Millennium Derwen

Penrhos Farm, Llantilio Crossenny, Monmouthshire.

Access: At all times.

From Penrhos Farm, at a fork in the lanes, a mile south of Llantilio Crossenny, take the public footpath eastwards through the orchards for almost half a mile.

Parking near Penrhos Farm is very limited.

(p.56 / map E5)

⑫ Crickhowell Black Poplars

Next to the old bridge over the River Usk at Crickhowell, Powys.

Access: the trees are on the private land of Glanusk Park Estate, but are readily viewable from the parapet of the bridge and adjoining roads.

(p.58 / map D5)

⑬ The Weird Birches of Ty-uchaf

On open pasture land near Llanelly, Monmouthshire.

Access: At all times (with consideration).

Take the lane westwards out of the village of Llanelly.

After 1 mile turn right at T-junction. After half a mile turn right, going down hill. After about 400 yards a rough track forks right off the road. Park here and walk another 400 yards along the track until you see a stile on the right.

Once over this, head into the fields in a south-westerly direction until you see the trees.

N.b. This is private land, but the owners are happy for visitors to view the trees.

Please park vehicles responsibly, shut all gates behind you and keep dogs on leads.

(p.60 / map D5)

Gazetteer (14–37)

14 Ty-uchaf Wall Ash

On open pasture land near Llanelly, Monmouthshire.

Access: At all times (with consideration).

Directions – as above, but after crossing the stile follow the green lane (between the dry stone walls) and the tree will be found in the wall after about 200 yards.

Conditions of access – as above.

(p.64 / map D5)

15 Least or Lesser Whitebeam

On the cliff edges of Craig y Cilau, above Llangattock, Powys.

Access: At all times (with care).

Take the hill road up out of Llangattock, heading west. After about 1.5 miles park on the roadside lay-by and strike off to the left (south), up on to the hills. The trees grow along the top of the crags.

(p.66 / map D5)

16 Welsh Whitebeam

On cliffs above old quarries at Pantydarren, south-west of Llanelly, Monmouthshire.

Access: At all times (with care).

Take the westward lane out of Llanelly and after 1 mile turn left at the T-junction. The trees will be found on the cliffs on the right side of the road after about half a mile.

(p.70 / map D5)

17 Ty Mawr Oak

On a private estate south of Abergavenny, Monmouthshire.

Access: Unfortunately no access currently permitted to this tree.

(p.72 / map D6)

18 The Blorenge Beeches

At various places all over the Blorenge hill to the south-west of Abergavenny, Monmouthshire.

Access: At all times.

Take the steep, narrow lane that branches right off the B4269, just south of Llanfoist, turning right after about a mile, and right again after several hundred yards. After a bit less than a mile, where the road becomes unfenced, park near a small plantation of conifers, and walk eastwards down the public footpath to the Punchbowl.

You will soon discover amazing beeches.

(p.74 / map D6)

19 Llangattock-juxta-Usk Yew

In the wall of St. Cadoc's churchyard, Llangattock-juxta-Usk, Monmouthshire.

Access: At all times.

Llangattock-juxta-Usk is immediately to the south of the A40, about 3 miles south-east of Abergavenny.

(p.78 / map D6)

20 Bettws Newydd Yew

In St. Aeddan's churchyard, Bettws Newydd, Monmouthshire.

Access: At all times.

The village is on a minor road about 4 miles north of Usk.

(p.80 / map D6)

21 Monmouthshire Orchards

To be found in various parts of the county.

Access: All orchards are on private land so, as a matter of courtesy, if you wish to view please ask permission from individual owners.

(p.82 / map E6)

22 Charley Trees

To be found in various parts of Wales, but most frequently along the English borders.

Access: Usually viewable from a public highway.

(p.92)

23 Monmouth Catalpa

St. James Square, Monmouth.

Access: At all times.

(p.94 / map E6)

24 Caeryder Oak

Near the village of Llanhennock, near Caerleon, Monmouthshire.

Access: The tree stands in a private field next to the road, opposite Pencraig Farm.

(p.98 / map D6)

25 Curley Oak

The tree stands within dense conifer forestry in Wentwood Forest, Newport.

Access: At all times.

This is a difficult tree to find.

From Parc Seymour, just north of the A48 east of Newport, take the country lane through the forest towards Pen-y-cae-mawr.

Approx. 2 miles up this road take the broad well-made forestry track on the left. After about half a mile where the wood stops on the left, walk down into the woodland and you should find the oak.

(p.102 / map E6)

Chepstow Aspen

In the middle of the golf course at St. Pierre Hotel and Country Club, off the A48, south of Chepstow, Monmouthshire.

Access: Open during daylight hours; ample car parking next to the hotel and country club.

Take the public footpath, running parallel with the entrance drive for about half a mile. Where it swings down to the left, cross the fairways (stay vigilant) and the aspen 'wood' is straight ahead.

(p.104 / map E6)

 Pontypool Sweet Chestnuts

Pontypool Park, Pontypool, Torfaen.

Access: At all times.

The park is easily located to the east of the town centre, and there are several gates.

The chestnuts are found in the valley in the middle of the park, between the rugby ground and the dry ski slope.

(p.106 / map D6)

 Mamhilad Yew

In St. Illtyd's churchyard, Mamhilad, Monmouthshire.

Access: At all times.

About 3 miles north-east of Pontypool, off the A4042.

(p.108 / map D6)

 Bute Park

In the centre of the city of Cardiff

Access: Opening times – daily from about 7.30am until dusk.

(p.112 / map D6)

 True Service Tree

On the sea cliffs at East, Aberthaw Vale of Glamorgan.

Access: Through Fontygary Leisure Park (ask permission at reception), go to the western most point in the park, where a footpath leads down on to the beach. Turn eastwards and the trees will be seen on the cliff face.

(p.118 / map D7)

 **Silent Valley Beeches**

The valley lies 2.5 miles south of Ebbw Vale.

Access: At all times.

Leave the A4046 just north of Cwm and turn into the village.

Look for the left turning with a brown tourist sign. Take this turning up the hill and after 400 yards there is a car park on the right. Walk across a grass playing area and into the woods.

(p.122 / map D6)

 Ley's Whitebeam

On cliff edges on Penmoelallt, on the west side, and on Darren Fach on the east side of the Taff Valley, north of Merthyr Tydfil.

Access: At all times. Extremely difficult to find and located in very precipitous situations (with great care).

(p.124 / map D6)

 Llangorse Wych Elm

In pasture to the north-west of Llangorse, Powys.

Access: at all times (with consideration).

Near the south end of Llangorse village, at a little grass triangle, take the left fork up a minor road, and almost immediately fork left again. Follow the lane for about half a mile, and where the lane takes a sharp turn right go through the gate facing you into the field. Turn right up the inside of the hedge and the elm will be found about 100 yards along.

N.b. This is private land, but the owners are happy for visitors to view the tree.

Please park vehicles responsibly, shut all gates behind you and keep dogs on leads.

(p.126 / map D5)

 Llanfeugan Yew Circle

In St. Meugan's churchyard, Llanfeugan, Powys.

Access: At all times.

About 4 miles south-east of Brecon, above the village of Pencelli.

(p.128 / map D5)

 Brecon Black Poplar

On the edge of the playing fields of Christ College, Brecon, Powys.

Access: At all times.

The tree stands next to a public footpath, south of the river bridge, and to the west of the river, a little past the end of Dinas Road.

(p.130 / map D5)

 Rhandirmwyn Oak

On the roadside above Pwllpriddog Farm, Rhandirmwyn, Carmarthenshire.

Access: At all times.

(p.134 / map C5)

 Defynnog Yew

In St. Cynog's churchyard, Defynog, Powys.

Access: At all times.

About 1 miles south of Sennybridge.

(p.136 / map D5)

Gazetteer (38–64)

 Talley Abbey Ash

In a hedgerow near Talley Abbey (Cadw), Carmarthenshire.

Access: At all times.

From the abbey car park walk through the adjacent churchyard and out of the far gate. Follow the path alongside a hedge for about 200 yards and the ash cannot be missed as it is right on the path.

Talley Abbey is about 6 miles north of Llandeilo, along the B4302.

(p.138 / map C5)

 Dinefwr Oaks

In Dinefwr Park, surrounding Newton House (National Trust), Llandeilo, Carmarthenshire.

Access: Check with National Trust for opening times.

Admission charges apply to the house, but not the park. The park is immediately west of Llandeilo.

(p.140 / map C5)

 Golden Grove

Various remarkable conifers in the arboretum (Carmarthenshire County Council)

Access: Opening times April – September 10.30 – 5.00pm

October – March 10.30 – 4.00pm

Ample car parking with small charge.

The Country Park and Arboretum are about 4 miles south-west of Llandeilo, just south of the B4300.

(p.144 / map C5)

 Aberglasney Yew Tunnel

In the gardens of Aberglasney House, Llangathen, Carmarthenshire.

Access: Check with Aberglasney Restoration Trust for opening times.

Admission charges apply.

Ample car parking.

Aberglasney is approx. 4 miles west of Llandeilo.

(p.146 / map C5)

 Ramsey Island Junipers

Four trees on cliffs along the east side of the island.

Access: At any time, but with extreme caution.

Please seek the advice and assistance of the RSPB warden.

Ramsey Island is off the west coast of Pembrokeshire, near St. David's.

(p.150 / map A5)

 **The Bleeding Yew of Nevern**

In St. Brynach's churchyard, Nevern, Pembrokeshire.

Access: At all times.

Nevern lies on the B4582, about 8 miles east of Fishguard.

(p.154 / map B5)

 Laburnum Hedges of Ceredigion

All over Ceredigion, but particularly good around the villages of Pentregat and Penrhiw-pâl, north of Newcastle Emlyn,
Access: At all times.

Many hedges are viewable from public road and rights of way.

(p.156 / map B5)

 Strata Florida Yews

At Strata Florida Abbey (Cadw), Ceredigion.

Access: At all times.

The Abbey lies about 1 mile east of Pontrhydfendigaid on the B4343.

(p.160 / map C4)

 Ystrad Meurig Ash

By the roadside in the village of Ystrad Meurig, Ceredigion.

Access: The tree is on private land, but can be viewed through the hedge on the south side of the road.

(p.164 / map C4)

 Hafod Beeches

There are many fine beeches throughout the Hafod Estate, Ceredigion (Hafod Trust & Forestry Commission).

Access: At all times. Limited car parking at signed car park south of B4574, between Cwmystwyth and Pont-rhyd-y-groes.

Hafod is about 10 miles east of Aberystwyth.

(p.166 / map C4)

 Prostrate Blackthorn

On Tanybwlch beach, immediately south of Aberystwyth, Ceredigion.

Access: At all times.

(p.170 / map C4)

Petrified Forest at Borth

The tree stumps may be seen in the sands between Borth and Ynyslas at low tide. Ceredigion.

Access: At all times.

Park in the large car park where the Ynyslas road forks off the B4353, hop over the sea wall and you should find plenty of trees.

(p.172 / map C4)

Mallwyd Yew

In St. Tydecho's churchyard, Mallwyd, Gwynedd.

Access: At all times.

Mallwyd is about 12 miles east of Dolgellau, where the A470 meets the A458.

(p.176 / map C3)

 **Lone Yew of Llynierth**

The tree is on a small mound at the southern end of Bala Lake, Gwynedd.

Access: since this is private land the best way to view the tree is from the lake.

(p.178 / map C3)

 Llanddeiniolen Yews

In St. Deiniolen's churchyard, Llanddeiniolen, Gwynedd.

Access: At all times.

Deiniolen is about 5 miles south of Bangor on a minor road.

(p.180 / map C2)

Bodnant Laburnum Arch

In the gardens of Bodnant (National Trust), Conwy.

Access: Check with National Trust for opening times.

Admission charges apply.

(p.182 / map C2)

Llangernyw Yew

In St. Digain's churchyard, Llangernyw, Conwy.

Access: At all times.

Llangernyw lies on the A548, mid way between Abergele and Llanrwst.

(p.186 / map C2)

Nantglyn Yew

In St. James' churchyard, Nantglyn, Denbighshire.

Access: At all times.

Nantglyn is on the B5435, about 5 miles south-west of Denbigh.

(p.188 / map D2)

Three Sisters Sweet Chestnuts

In a private garden on the A525, main Ruthin to Denbigh road, near Pentre-Llanrhaeadr, Denbighshire.

Access: No public access to this tree.

(p.190 / map D2)

 The Peace Tree

In the village square in the centre of Caerwys, Flintshire.

Access: At all times

(p.192 / map D2)

 Gresford Yew

In All Saints' churchyard, Gresford, Wrexham.

Access: At all times.

(p.196 / map D2)

 **Overton-on-Dee Yews**

In St. Mary the Virgin churchyard, Overton-on-Dee, Wrexham.

Access: At all times.

(p.200 / map E2)

 **Llangollen Whitebeam**

On the crags of the Eglwyseg Valley, nr Llangollen, Denbighshire.

Access: At all times (with extreme care)

The crags are above minor roads about 3 miles north of Llangollen.

(p.202 / map D2)

 Pontfadog Oak

On private ground above the village of Pontfadog, Wrexham.

Access: Only by special appointment through The Tree Council 020 7407 9992.

(p.208 / map D2)

Great Oak at the Gates of the Dead

In scrub vegetation 2 miles west of Chirk, Wrexham.

Access: May be viewed from the roadside or a permissive path which runs through the woods behind the tree.

It is just north of the B4500, immediately before a left turn to Bronygarth.

(p.210 / map D2)

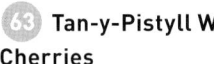 **Tan-y-Pistyll Wild Cherries**

On field boundaries to the south of the lane, just short of Tan-y-Pistyll, Powys.

Access: Private land, but the trees are viewable from the nearby lane.

From Llanrhaeadr-ym-Mochnant take the narrow lane signposted to Pistyll Rhaeadr (waterfall). About half a mile before the waterfall the cherries are in a field to the left.

(p.212 / map D3)

Pennant Melangell Yews

In St. Melangell's churchyard, Pennant Melangell, Powys.

Access: At all times.

Turn west off the B4391 at Llangynog and follow the narrow lane about 2 miles to the end where you will find the church.

(p.216 / map D3)

Gazetteer (65–74)

The Patriarch Tree

In St. Erfyl's churchyard, Llanerfyl, Powys.

Access: At all times.

The village is on the A458 about 12 miles west of Welshpool.

(p.220 / map D3)

Buttington Oak

In the fields to the east of the River Severn, north of Buttington, Powys.

Access: A public footpath runs through the fields to the oak.

Take the A458 towards Shrewsbury from the roundabout north of Welshpool, cross the River Severn, and almost immediately a gate on the left leads into the wide open pastures. The tree is about half a mile to the north.

(p.222 / map D3)

Buttington Yew

In All Saints' churchyard, Buttington, Powys.

Access: At all times.

The village lies on the A458, about 2 miles north-east of Welshpool.

(p.224 / map D3)

 Powis Castle Estate Oaks

On the Powis Castle Estate parklands, Welshpool, Powys.

Access: The estate is private, but the trees featured in this book may be viewed from the approach and exit roads to the castle.

Gwen Morgan's Oak stands about 200 yards from the castle, down the exit drive, on the right, just over the cattle grid.

(p.226 / map D3)

69 Yews of Powis Castle

In the gardens of Powis Castle (National Trust), Welshpool, Powys.

Access: Check with National Trust for opening times.

Admission charges apply.

(p.230 / map D3)

70 Charles Ackers' Redwood Grove

The Grove lies to the east of the B4388 on hills above the Leighton Estate, about a mile north of the village of Kingswood.

Access: The Grove belongs to the Royal Forestry Society, and permission to visit must be sought through them.

(p.234 / map D3)

71 Garthmyl Oak

Near the village of Garthmyl, Powys.

Access: The tree is on private land, but special permission to visit may be sought through The Tree Council – 020 7407 9992.

Garthmyl is on the A483, mid way between Newtown and Welshpool.

(p.238 / map D3)

Garthmyl Cedar of Lebanon

The tree is in the grounds of Garthmyl Hall, Garthmyl, Powys.

Access: Although the tree is on private land the owners have kindly given permission for people to visit, but have stipulated that anyone doing so must introduce themselves at the house first.

The Hall is up a drive to the west of the A483, just before entering the village.

(p.240 / map D3)

73 Newtown Black Poplar

Unmissable as it stands in the main municipal car park in the centre of Newtown, Powys.

Access: At all times.

(p.242 / map D4)

74 Dolfor Sentinel Yews

On the hills south of Newtown, Powys.

Access: On private farm land.

The trees are viewable from the road.

About 3 miles south of Newtown, and less than a mile north of Dolfor, on the A483, the trees may be seen on the hillside to the east of the road near a lay-by.

(p.244 / map D4)

The Tree Council

The Tree Council is the UK's lead charity for trees in all settings, urban and rural, promoting their importance in a changing environment and it works in partnership with communities, organisations and government to make trees matter to everyone. It was launched in 1974 to run the annual **National Tree Week** and act as a forum for lobbying and debate, building on the success of **National Tree Planting Year** with its slogan, **Plant A Tree In '73**. The movement has developed to encompass community action, lobbying, awareness raising and grant giving. Members of The Tree Council now range from professional, non-governmental, specialist and trade organisations, including other conservation charities, to government departments and local authorities. Those individuals who show an interest in becoming actively involved with tree planting, care and conservation are encouraged to become Tree Wardens; they may also join one of The Tree Council's constituent organisations.

The annual national programme of community action and awareness-raising around trees has grown over the years to become a major part of the work of this organisation. In addition to **National Tree Week**, launched at the end of November each year, The Tree Council also organises and promotes **Seed Gathering Season** during September and October and **Walk in the Woods** month throughout May, supporting the groups organising local events; all these initiatives are aimed at involving as many people as possible in planting, caring for and enjoying trees and woods and their timing reflects the seasons of the tree year.

Working with partners, member organisations and Tree Wardens, The Tree Council is active on particular issues of concern such as **Hedgerow Harvest**, extending fruiting hedgerow networks; improving the numbers of **Hedge Trees**; and the **Tree Care Campaign** for after-care to increase the survival rates of young trees. The **Green Monument Campaign**, a drive for proper recognition for heritage trees, was launched in 2003 to achieve effective safeguards, resources for custodians to promote their wellbeing and access to information on management best practice. In 1995, when the Llangernyw Yew with its 11m girth was identified as being up to 4,000 years old and therefore the oldest tree in Wales, The Tree Council grant funded the removal of an old oil tank from the centre hollow of the trunk and brought the spotlight to bear on the tree as part of the National Tree Week celebrations. Since that time, tree stories from across the UK have been collected and published in a series of books of which this is the fifth, though the first to concentrate on Wales, with the intention of celebrating and recording trees that are central to the historical and cultural heritage of each nation.

More information can be found on The Tree Council's website
www.treecouncil.org.uk

**Cyngor Cefn Gwlad Cymru
Countryside Council for Wales**

Countryside Council for Wales

The Countryside Council for Wales (CCW) is the Welsh Government's statutory adviser on sustaining the landscape's natural beauty, protecting wildlife and promoting opportunities for everyone to enjoy the outdoors.

CCW champions the environment of Wales as a source of natural and cultural riches, as a foundation for economic and social activity, and as a place for leisure and learning opportunities.

Our aim is to make the environment a valued part of everyone's life in Wales.

CCW's guiding principle is that the environment is our life support system – vital for the survival and wellbeing of all forms of life.

The benefits derived from trees are numerous and fundamentally important. They provide:

- rich habitats for wildlife – veteran trees are particularly rich in wildlife;

- timber for buildings, furniture and fuel;

- help in tackling climate change, through locking in massive amounts of carbon in timber and woodland soils that would otherwise be released into the atmosphere;

- purification of the air we breathe, and management of our water resources;

- amazing places for recreation,

CCW manages some of Wales' most precious woodlands as National Nature Reserves – you are welcome to visit and enjoy them.

More information can be found on CCW's website **www.ccw.gov.uk**

Forestry Commission Wales

A total of 14.3 per cent of Wales is covered by woodlands. Of this, 38% (126,000 hectares/311,000 acres) is owned by the Welsh Government. Forestry Commission Wales is the Welsh Government's department of forestry and manages these woodlands on its behalf. In so doing, we aim to balance the needs of people, the environment and the forest economy, in line with the priorities of the Welsh Government's strategy, Woodlands for Wales.

On a landscape scale, woodlands and trees make a positive contribution to the special character of Wales, helping to define our most precious sites of heritage and cultural importance.

We believe that improving the condition and management of our woodlands is the key to healthy and resilient ecosystems, capable of delivering the high quality goods and services we need.

Shining brightly as jewels among our woodlands, Wales has a wealth of important individual trees with historic, cultural and environmental interest. The importance of ancient woodlands and veteran trees as a cultural heritage resource should not be under-estimated.

At Forestry Commission Wales, we recognise the value to society and the environment of our trees, particularly veteran trees, and strive to manage them for their biodiversity, landscape, heritage and cultural value.

More information can be found on the Forestry Commission's website **www.forestry.gov.uk/wales**

Bibliography

Robert Bevan-Jones – *The Ancient Yew – A History of Taxus baccata* Windgather Press 2002

J.E. Bowman – *Magazine of Natural History* 1833

Vaughan Cornish, D.Sc. – *The Churchyard Yew and Immortality* Frederick Muller 1946

Archdeacon Coxe – *Historical Tour of Monmouth* 1799

William Barker Daniel – *Rural Sports* 1813

H.J. Elwes and A. Henry – *The Trees of Great Britain and Ireland Edinburgh* 1907–13

Richard Fenton – *Tours in Wales* 1810

William Gilpin – *Essay on Picturesque Beauty* 1792

Geoffrey Grigson – *The Englishman's Flora* Phoenix House/J.M. Dent 1987

Fred Hageneder – *Yew, A History* Sutton Publishing 2007

Esmond Harris, Jeanette Harris and N.D.G. James – *Oak, A British History* Windgather Press 2003

William Hone – *The Every-day Book* 1830

H.A. Hyde, M.A., F.L.S. – *Welsh Timber Trees Native and Introduced* National Museum of Wales and The Press Board of the University of Wales 1935 (2nd edn.)

E. Hyde Hall – *A Description of Caernarvonshire* 1809/11

G. S. Jarman – *The Village of Gresford* 1912

Rev. C.A. Johns, B.A., F.L.S. – *The Forest Trees of Britain* 1849

Hugh Johnson – *Trees* Mitchell Beazley 2010

Dr. Owen Johnson – *Champion Trees of Britain and Ireland* Published by Royal Botanic Gardens Kew 2011

John Leland – *Itinerary* 1538

Samuel Lewis – *A Topographical Dictionary of Wales* 1833

William Linnard – *Welsh Woods and Forests, A History* Gomer Press 2000

John Claudius Loudon – *Arboretum et Fruticetum Britannicum* Longman, Brown, Green and Longmans (1838)

Archie Miles – *The Hidden Trees of Britain* Ebury Press 2007

Archie Miles – *A Walk in the Woods* Francis Lincoln 2009

Edward Mogg – *Paterson's Roads* 1829 (18th edn.)

Monthly magazine or British register – Vol.39 1815

Joan Morgan and Alison Richards – *The New Book of Apples* Ebury Press 2002 (revised edn.)

Nennius – *Historia Britonnum* 829

The Orthodox Churchman's Magazine; or a Treasury of Divine and Useful Knowledge 1801

Thomas Pennant – *A Tour in Wales* 1781

Thomas Pennant – *The Tour in North Wales* 1783

Tim Rich, Libby Houston, Ashley Robertson and Michael Proctor – *Whitebeams, Rowans and Service Trees of Britain and Ireland* BSBI 2010

Donald Rodger, Jon Stokes and James Ogilvie – *Heritage Trees of Scotland* Forestry Commission Scotland and The Tree Council 2006

Jon Stokes and Donald Rodger – *The Heritage Trees of Britain and Northern Ireland* Constable 2004

Richard Warner – *A Second walk through Wales* 1798

Index (A-M)

Index (M–Y)

Acknowledgements

My journey through the treescapes of Wales, visiting some of the most dramatic and beautiful locations, to find the trees within these pages, has been a pleasure and a privilege. All the encouragement and advice that I received from the many tree owners and enthusiasts along the way helped to make it a very happy and fruitful adventure, and I hope that I have not forgotten anyone, but please forgive me if I have.

You know who you are

A very special mention must go to my partner Jan who happily endures my late nights at the keyboard and hideously early morning departures for photography.

Huge appreciation goes to all the following people, for their generosity with their time and knowledge, for their permission to photograph and include their trees, and without whom this book would not have been possible.

Jon Stokes and **Pauline Buchanan Black** at The Tree Council

Hilary Miller at Countryside Council for Wales

Judith Webb and **Sam Argent** at Forestry Commission Wales

Edward Parker and **Katherine Owen** of Ancient Tree Hunt, Woodland Trust

Ray Hawes at National Trust

Dr. Tim Rich at National Museum Wales

Tim Hills and all his colleagues at The Ancient Yew Group

David Alderman at The Tree Register

David Matthews at the Welsh Perry and Cider Society

Alice Britt at Gwent Wildlife Trust

Tom Till of Powis Castle Estate

Matthew Wride and **Jon Green** at Bute Park, Cardiff Council

Keith Williams and **Mike Smith** at Golden Grove, Carmarthenshire County Council

Phil Grimes of Torfaen Borough County Council

Greg Morgan, RSPB Warden on Ramsey Island

Tony Glacken for his sensitive handling of my original text.

David L. Williams at Peter Gill & Associates for his excellent design.

Matthew Howard at Graffeg for his attention to detail and bearing with me.

Peter Gill for his enthusiasm for the project and for publishing the book.

Joseph Atkin (Head Gardener – Aberglasney); The Baker family; Shaun Burkey; Arthur Chater; Sue Chivers (Monmouth Action Group); Christine Churchill; Steve Clarke (Monmouth Archaeology); Stephen Evans (B.S.B.I. Welsh Bulletin, 2003); Heather Ewers; Phillip Facey (Pistyll Rhaeadr); Liz Fleming-Williams; Fontygary Leisure Park; Rory Francis (Woodland Trust); Mr and Mrs B. Hughes; Julia Johnson; Penri Jones; Thomas Jones; Mr and Mrs S. Liney; Rob McBride (Tree Hunter); Jacqui Mitchell (National Trust – Dinefwr Park); Ross and Elizabeth Murray; Revd. Lynette D. Norman; Anna Orton and David Swanton (National Trust – Powis Castle); Mr and Mrs Owen; John Phillips; Ynyr and Eurig Roberts ("Brigyn"); Troy Smith (National Trust – Bodnant); Jeff Thomas, Adrian and Lorna Foster (www.castlewales.com); Tony at Neath website design; author photo. by Jan Trewin; The Watkins family; Mr and Mrs G. Watkins; John White; Linos Jones Williams; Tim Winter; Christian Wolf; Nigel Young (www.caerleon.net).

Archive images

National Library of Wales – 17, 20, 31, 100, 169, 193, 194; Tim Winter Collection – 21, 22, 24 (left), 25 (top), 29 (right), 142; David Alderman Collection/The Tree Register – 25 (bottom); Natural History Museum – 27; Neath Website Design (original source of image unknown, usage gratefully acknowledged) – 29 (left); National Museum Wales – 32; Courtesy Mrs. Julia Johnson – 54; Nigel Young (www.caerleon.net) – 99; Courtesy Dr. Tim Rich – 124; Liz Fleming-Williams – 134; Christian Wolf Collection – 163, 220; All other archive images – Archie Miles Collection.